1988

To the College
Library of the College
of Saint Francis

with Best wishes
from Kathleen L. Kirван

STUDIES IN GERMAN LITERATURE,
LINGUISTICS, AND CULTURE

VOL. 14

STUDIES IN GERMAN LITERATURE, LINGUISTICS, AND CULTURE

VOL. 14

CAMDEN HOUSE
Columbia, South Carolina

PATTERN AND CHAOS

PATTERN AND CHAOS

Multilinear Novels by
Dos Passos
Döblin
Faulkner and
Koeppen

KATHLEEN L. KOMAR

CAMDEN HOUSE
Columbia, South Carolina

Set in Garamond type
and printed on acid-free
Glatfelder paper.

Copyright ©1983 by Camden House, Inc.
Drawer 2025
Columbia, South Carolina 29202

Acknowledgments

I WOULD LIKE TO express my gratitude to the American Council of Learned Societies and the Academic Senate of the University of California at Los Angeles, both of which provided grants which made the research in this manuscript possible. I would also like to thank *The German Quarterly* for allowing me to reprint parts of the article "Technique and Structure in Döblin's *Berlin Alexanderplatz*," (*GQ*, May 1981, LIV, 3, pp. 318-334); and *Faulkner Studies* for allowing me to reprint parts of "A Structural Study of *As I Lay Dying*," (*Faulkner Studies* I, 1980, pp. 48-57).

I am also grateful to the following publishers and individuals for their kind permission to use the photos which appear in this volume: for the Dos Passos photo, *The Fourteenth Chronicle: Letters and Diaries of John Dos Passos*, edited by Townsend Ludington, photograph courtesy of Elizabeth H. Dos Passos, by permission of Gambit Publishers, Inc., copyright 1973 by Elizabeth H. Dos Passos and Townsend Ludington; for the Faulkner photo, *Selections from the William Faulkner Collection of Louis Daniel Brodsky: A Descriptive Catalogue*, edited by Louis Daniel Brodsky and Robert W. Hamblin, photograph courtesy of Louis Daniel Brodsky, by permission of University Press of Virginia, copyright 1979; for the Döblin photo, *Alfred Döblin Autobiographische Schriften und letzte Aufzeichnungen*, edited by Edgar Pässler, Walter-Verlag AG, copyright, 1977; for the Koeppen photo, *Kindlers Literaturgeschichte der Gegenwart—Autoren, Werke, Themen, Tendenzen seit 1945*, edited by Heinrich Vormweg, Kindler Verlag GmbH, copyright 1973.

K.L.K.
October 1982

CONTENTS

I
Introduction

THE AESTHETIC EXPERIMENTS of early twentieth-century writers and artists represent an explosion of artistic techniques which has had repercussions to the present day. One of the most popular of those techniques is the surface fragmentation of a literary text accompanied by the embedding of more coherent patterns at a deeper level. Any reader contemplating contemporary literature is struck by the frequent appearance of novels in which the narrative text is fragmented, split up into several separate (and often seemingly unrelated) lines of narration, a form characteristic of the works of Joyce, Dos Passos and Faulkner. In *Katz und Maus*, for example, Günther Grass fragments and reshuffles the chronological sequence of Mahlke's story while juxtaposing to it the story of the psychological development of the narrator Pilenz. An even more striking example of the technique of multiple lines of narration is Heinrich Böll's *Gruppenbild mit Dame* in which he focuses on the problem of multiple narration and authorial objectivity by providing a narrator, the "Verf.[asser]," who is himself a character with a limited point-of-view which is paralleled by the narrations of other "informants." Böll writes an author into his work so that he can act out the dilemma of a limited narrative consciousness faced with an ambiguous picture presented from multiple points-of-view. This structural fragmentation and multiplicity also occurs in novels by such German writers as Hermann Broch, Heimito von Doderer, Wolfgang Koeppen, Uwe Johnson, and others. American novelists such as John Dos Passos, William Faulkner, Djuna Barnes, John Hawkes, Joseph Heller, and

Thomas Pynchon, and in France Natalie Sarraute and André Gide, or in Latin America Carlos Fuentes and Gabriel Garcia Marquez make use of this same fragmented narrative structure. The prominence of this novelistic form in the Twentieth Century provides the focus for this study.

My main goal is to investigate this literary sub-genre, which can be termed the multilinear novel, to describe its emergence, development and place in literary history. My method is to analyze closely the formal characteristics of the novels and, in particular, the coherent structures which underlie the fragmented surfaces of such multilinear texts. I am concerned with the way modern writers go about creating systems of meaning within each work, what units of meaning they produce and convey within an individual text to compensate for the lack of any shared system of meaning between themselves and their readership or even among individual readers. The investigation focuses, in part, on how the act of writing itself becomes the creating of a common order and the waging of a battle against the solipsism that constantly threatens modern consciousness because of the increased isolation and alienation of the dehumanized technological urban environment in which twentieth-century man finds himself.

In order to discover and understand those basic units of meaning particular to each text, my analysis concentrates on the structures specific to the individual text, while keeping in mind the common cultural problem to which all the texts are responding. I attempt to account systematically for the production of meaning by delineating the units that group together to form larger systems of implication. The nature of those basic units of meaning varies from work to work. Some authors rely heavily on the repetition and development of related symbols and images (as one would do in a poem) while others emphasize plot construction and still others the juxtaposition and interaction of character types. Any (or all) of these could serve as basic units of meaning in a particular text.

The grouping and interaction of these basic units create the structure of the text. The term "structure" here goes beyond the static arrangement we could designate simply as "form." To clarify the distinction, we can define the form of a Shakespearean sonnet as fourteen lines of iambic pentameter divided into three quatrains and a couplet, rhyming abab cdcd efef gg. But in doing so, we have not yet considered the dynamic interrelationship of those parts nor the tensions and implications created by the juxtaposition of particular images and themes. Therefore, we have stopped short of investigating its structure. Structure signifies that particular set of dynamic interrelations of basic units in a text which generates the tensions and creates the meanings at the heart of each literary work. Much of my investigation is "structural," therefore, in that it seeks to determine and delineate the units of meaning and the systems which enable the disparate readers of an individual text to perceive its meaning.

Having defined my preliminary set of interests in the multilinear genre and chosen a method which seemed appropriate to them, I had to select, from among a large number of possible novels, the individual texts on which my study would focus. I was interested in examining a range of possible formal responses to the chaotic fragmentation of the modern, twentieth-century world. I was also interested in looking at the genre during one of its periods of formative activity—that is, early in this century, specifically the period between the wars. My first three texts were selected on this basis. Dos Passos' *Manhattan Transfer*, Döblin's *Berlin Alexanderplatz*, and Faulkner's *As I Lay Dying* all consciously record in their literary surfaces the chaotic modern world of deteriorating individual and social values, while juxtaposing to that modern chaos a deeper structure of aesthetic order, but each text provides a different system of techniques for generating that underlying order. In order to add one further dimension to the study, I decided to select my last text from a somewhat later period thus enabling me to make at least tentative diachronic statements to supplement my synchronic conclusions. Koeppen's *Tauben im Gras* was chosen from among many possibilities because it shares with the earlier texts the basic themes of dissolution and chaos underpinned by a more subtle pattern of meaning and because of its striking similarity in strategy to Dos Passos' novel. I was curious to see if this reappearance of the basic multilinear model provided by Dos Passos could be accounted for either formally or culturally.

The novels also vary in the strength and meaning of their embedded systems of order. Dos Passos, for example, depicts a recurrence of events across the lives of individual characters, but the repetitive structure thus produced creates a kind of "statistical determinism"[1] that undermines meaning in individual lives rather than supporting it. Döblin, on the other hand, forcefully maintains a complex ordering system of allusion and interpolation in order to reveal and reinforce meaning and social integration for the individual. The four novels as a group, then, represent through their specific form a range of possible technical responses to a central philosophical dilemma of modern literature; they share the use of embedded structures to produce a multilinear work.

The present study to some extent seeks to enlarge and refine the typological studies of Lämmert, Stanzel, Beach, and others. It goes beyond the basic work of categorization to suggest possible links between individual structures and thematic interests, cultural enrivonment, and literary development.

The narrative sub-genre under consideration is not, of course, an entirely new phenomenon. In fact, the seeds of multilinearity and fragmented surface structures are inherent in the very beginnings of the novel form. If we go back to the forerunners of the modern novel, the Spanish picaresque tales such as *Lazarillo de Tormes* or even Cervantes' *Don Quixote*, we can already see the linking of individual episodes in a manner other than strictly causal relationships or linearity of plot. In *Don Quixote* we also have the dual point-of-view that demands that the reader constantly evaluate the visions of the main character as opposed to the more sober view of his fellow men. At no time, however, is the reader truly uncertain of where "reality" lies in the tale although he may well prefer the delusion of the Don to the reality which surrounds him.

This potential line of development for the novel is picked up in the Eighteenth Century by writers such as Laurence Sterne in *Tristram Shandy* or Diderot in *Jacques le Fataliste*. Sterne, for example, constantly interrupts his main narrative line to digress to apparently unrelated topics ranging from the exploits of his Uncle Toby to the graphically depicted development of his own plot in Book Five. In both Sterne and Diderot, the reader is drawn into the process of the telling of the tale and asked to participate rather than merely observe. These authors already focus on the impossibility of certain human aspirations. Tristram, for example, is constantly aware of the futility of the task of writing against his own death, of attempting to outrun in his narrative the reality which entraps him. The reader, however, while he may be confused or even frustrated in his attempt to read on along the main plot line, is never really radically disoriented. The world of the text is whimsical and extremely complex, but it plays itself out against a relatively stable social and moral background.

This strain of fragmented and complex narrative is carried forward in time by the German writers of the late Eighteenth and early Nineteenth Centuries such as Jean Paul, Friedrich Schlegel, and E.T.A. Hoffman. These German writers, however, begin to add a new dimension to the fragmentation and digression employed by their predecessors. Hoffmann offers perhaps the clearest example of the nature of this new step. In his *Der goldene Topf*, Hoffmann consistently maintains two parallel narrative lines—one representing the "real" bourgeois world of Veronica and a second representing the magical world of Serpentina and her father. Hoffmann deliberately attempts to confuse the reader as to the validity of each of these worlds. For example, he uses his most logically and rationally couched appeals in the service of the magical world while constantly questioning the stability of the more "normal" world. To be sure, the reader has been provided with enough details about "medicinal" cordials and tobacco to see the magical realm as psychological delusion or hallucination on Anselmus' part. And yet, with Lindhorst's intrusion into the frame of the narrative (its supposedly most "realistic" part) as the story closes, the reader is invited radically to question the rational limits of his "real" world. In short, by employing a multilinear technique, Hoffmann forces the reader to evaluate and delineate the nature of reality.

We can see, then, a development of the novel in the direction of the twentieth-century term "multilinearity." This particular development, however, does not represent the main stream of the novel before the Twentieth Century. Critics such as Ian Watt in his *Rise of the Novel* rightly point out that the main force of the novel in the Eighteenth Century developed from the line of DeFoe, Fielding, and Richardson rather than Sterne. The Nineteenth Century moves in the direction of realism and eventually naturalism rather than whimsy and imaginative fragmentation. The most familiar novels of the Eighteenth and Nineteenth Centuries depend on the omniscient narrator in his many guises. But early in this century, the multilinear form not only makes a reappearance but also becomes a truly dominant force in literary development and interest.

Such writers as James Joyce, Virginia Woolf, Alfred Döblin, John Dos Passos and many others were experimenting with fragmentary, multilinear structures of various types. Eberhard Lämmert described a type of novel which contains "Umstellen von ganzen Großabschnitten der Geschichte; Ausfächerung und Verzweigung der Geschichte in Einzelverläufe und—zustände; schließlich Aufsplitterung in disparate Erzählmomente."[2] ("Transposition of entire major sections of the story; fanning out and branching of the story into individual narrative processes and circumstances; finally splitting up into disparate narrative elements." [Translations are my own unless otherwise designated.]) Franz Stanzel further refines Lämmert's categories:

> Die Ausfächerung und Verzweigung der Erzählung in Einzelgeschichten kann den unterschiedlichsten Absichten dienen. Sie wird notwendig, wo es gilt, ein breites Panorama, das Sittenbild einer ganzen Epoche, zu zeichnen, wie es John Dos Passos mit seiner programmatisch betitelten Trilogie *USA* versucht. Von ganz anderer Art ist die Mehrgleisigkeit von Romanen, in welchen ein Geschehen gleichsam perspektivisch umkreist wird, indem nacheinander verschiedene Personen ihre persönliche Version dieses Geschehens erzählen, z.B. in Lawrence Durrells Tetralogie, genannt *Alexandria Quartet*, oder Gerd Gaisers *Schlußball*. Die Aufsplitterung der Geschichte in kaleidoskopartige Bildfolgen, die Segmentierung von Handlungsabläufen in zusammenhanglos dargestellten Bruchstücken ist besonders im neuesten Roman und in der Nachfolge von James Joyce mit recht verschiedenem Erfolg versucht worden, so auch von Virginia Woolf, Faulkner, John Dos Passos, dessen *Manhattan Transfer* hier als besonders auffälliges Beispiel erwähnt werden muß.[3]

> The fanning out and branching of the narration into individual stories can serve the most varied purposes. It is necessary when it is a question of depicting a broad panorama, the moral portrait of an entire epoch, as John Dos Passos attempts in his programmatically titled trilogy *USA*. Of an entirely different kind is the multilinearity of novels in which a story is, as it were, circled from various perspectives so that various people in succession tell their personal version of the events, for example, in Lawrence Durrell's tetralogy entitled *Alexandria Quartet* or Gerd Gaiser's *Schlußball*. The splitting up of the story into a kaleidoscopic series of images, the division of the course of events into disconnected fragments has been attempted, especially in the most recent novels and among the followers of James Joyce, with

varying degrees of success, so too by Virginia Woolf, Faulkner, and John Dos Passos, whose *Manhattan Transfer* must be mentioned as a particularly striking example.

Although Stanzel, Lämmert and others have designated and categorized the phenomenon of multilinearity in the twentieth-century novel, they stop short of extended analysis. Joseph Warren Beach offers a more ambitious study of various types of modern novels based on what he terms "abstract composition."[4] His investigation, however, is often limited to descriptions of different techniques. I hope to contribute in the present study a more detailed analysis of individual twentieth-century works that exemplify varieties of multilinearity as well as to investigate what the twentieth-century version of the multilinear text adds to the earlier experiments of the Eighteenth and Nineteenth Centuries.

A novelist could produce a multilinear work by several different methods. He could, as Dos Passos does in *Manhattan Transfer* and as Koeppen does in *Tauben im Gras*, juxtapose several plot lines, the stories of many different characters who are largely unrelated to one another in any physical or logical way. This technique would produce a multilinearity of plot itself. A writer could also multiply the number of narrators as Faulkner does in *As I Lay Dying*, *The Sound and the Fury*, and *Absalom, Absalom!*. In this case the reader encounters a number of variations on a single basic story with the conflicting points-of-view of the narrators creating a larger plot of its own. Or one could multiply the number of narrative voices as Joyce does in *Ulysses* or Döblin in *Berlin Alexanderplatz*. In this multilinear structure not all the narrative voices are represented by physical characters within the frame of the dramatic action (as they are in Faulkner's *As I Lay Dying*). In fact, the reader is frequently at a loss to identify the narrator at all. Or one could produce multilinearity by echoing the action of the basic plot line in various systems of allusions or interpolated stories, thus reinforcing and commenting upon the main action as Döblin does in *Berlin Alexanderplatz*. The multilinearity of these fragmented novels may, therefore, take place on any of several different levels. My four choices are a representative sampling of the various structural possibilities.

Multilinearity, as a structural innovation, was not, of course, a case of spontaneous generation, popping onto the literary scene with no recognizable antecedents or nurturing medium. Works of this sort appeared, rather, at a time when the decline of dominant nineteenth-century narrative techniques—in particular the use of an omniscient narrator and the implied causality of chronological sequences —was leaving certain of the more formally progressive twentieth-century novelists with a paucity of acceptable and serviceable techniques and structures. For these narrative experimenters of the early Twentieth Century, the realistic tradition that had dominated the novel begins to give way to multilinearity in its various forms.

To have said so much, however, is to describe the formal evolution of the novel without designating the causes behind the exhaustion of one form and its replacement by another. It is not just that a particular literary technique becomes overworked; it is also that the technique or form ceases to correspond to the contemporary view of the world, which, after all, is the definition of the "overworking" of a technique. The older forms by their own obsolescence then become a challenge to new creation.

In the latter half of the Nineteenth Century the concept of the omniscient narrator, which had served several generations of novelists, began to be directly and vigorously questioned. In France, Flaubert called for the "impassibilité" of the author, proposing that natural events can tell their own story better than any intrusive narrator, while Henry James in England demanded the narrative perspective of a limited "center of consciousness" within the dramatic framework of the narrative, and Spielhagen in Germany called more drastically for the "execution of the narrator." These comments manifest a radical move away from the omniscient narrator.[5]

If we venture, briefly, beyond the realm of aesthetics, we find a cultural climate that left early twentieth-century writers no choice but to question the absolute authorial control and wisdom implied by the use of an omniscient narrator. On the social scene a major shift occurred in the lives of the twentieth-century writer and his readers. The eighteenth- and nineteenth-century novels were generally constructed upon a recognizable system of social order and behavior shared by writers and readers. The correctness of any social action and its consequences were relatively stable and the significance of a social gesture was evident to all who witnessed it. Marriages, deaths, shifts in social class, political and economic activities all formed part of an ordered system which was familiar enough to writer and reader to be taken for granted. The sense of comfortable agreement on the rightness and value of things is evident not only in the direct assurances of future justice an author might make to his reader in the course of a novel but also in the recognizability of good or bad types in character presentation. The major human interactions were firmly grounded in stable public institutions that had developed over long periods of time and had all the support of tradition. The social world both defined and then verified the value systems of the individuals who participated in it.

For writers of the early Twentieth Century, however, the stability of this social orientation and frequently even the social institutions themselves had disappeared. The common agreement about the value and magnitude of actions and their consequences had broken down. The public patterns of behavior had given way to myriad individual responses to an increasingly impersonal and confusing modern reality. The community of beliefs that had formerly defined a coherent society had given way to varied individual evaluations of a chaotic external world. Not only had religious continuity long since ceased to exist but the more basic moral agreement on the viability of "good" or "right" actions in the social and political arena had also disappeared. The public consensus on public actions had largely broken down. The rituals and traditional social forms that earlier novelists had relied upon as a common basis for themselves and their readers had deteriorated to a point where the author could no longer make any easy assumption of continuity in either his real or his fictional worlds. Many writers, as Thomas Mann points out in his *Zauberberg*, saw the First World War as the final watershed which divided them forever from the comfortable social forms of the past and which robbed them forever of the ability to depend on a readership with a consensus of moral, social, and public beliefs. The external world would no longer be so predictably aligned with the internal world of man.

The reasons for the shifts in social continuity in the early Twentieth Century can be found in a number of different areas. In economics, social theory and ethics thinkers were radically revising their ideas. Older forms of progressive thinking were being replaced by ideas of recurrence and circularity. Culturally jarring ideas were developing in the fields of science, psychology and philosophy.[6]

In these last areas, three theories in particular produced radical effects on writers and their works—Bergson's concepts of *durée* and *simultanéité*, Freud's ideas of the subconscious, and Einstein's theory of relativity. They undermined the earlier cultural attitudes toward temporal and spatial arrangements, causality, and the possibility of even positing any absolute, of which our relative views represent failed glimpses. These new philosophical, psychological, and physical theories leave twentieth-century man with the disconcerting dilemma of having to rethink his entire system of conceptualization and the forms of art that arise from it. The far-reaching effects of this situation were described in 1923 by Ortega y Gasset, who can serve as a representative witness for the impact of this well documented and now familiar revolution of consciousness:

> Let us imagine a moment of transition during which the great goals that yesterday furnished our landscape with so definite an architecture have been deprived of their lustre, of their attractive power and of their authority over us, while at the same time those that are destined to replace them have not yet acquired complete clarity of outline and competent vigour of growth. At such a season the landscape in the neighbourhood of the observer seems to break up, vacillate and quake in all directions....
>
> Such is the situation with which European existence is confronted today. The system of values by which its activity was regulated thirty years ago has lost its convincing character, its attractive force and its imperative vigour. The man of the

West is undergoing a process of radical disorientation because he no longer knows by what stars he is able to guide his life.[7]

This feeling of disorientation and crisis, of earlier structures dissolving in the face of new intellectual discoveries, triggered a search for new aesthetic forms more consistent with the new theories. This search is evident in the surge of aesthetic developments in the first thirty years of the century. Between 1905 and 1915 the Fauves, the Cubists, and the Expressionists emerged in the realm of painting. Marinetti's "Futurist Manifesto" appeared in 1910; T.S. Eliot began "Prufrock" in 1910; Kafka began *Der Prozess* and Joyce began *Ulysses* in 1914. The older aesthetic attitudes, built upon a kind of community of accepted beliefs, upon universal ordering principles and universally accepted absolutes, had crumbled. The modern artist is confronted with the problem of creating a comprehensible system of aesthetic meaning without the aid of external frameworks of order.

Perhaps the most devastating and, at the same time, most optimistic of the new theories is that of Einstein. It calls into question not the valdity of individual observations of reality, but the very nature of reality itself, viewed by earlier ages as some abstract absolute. Ortega y Gasset elaborates on this essential innovation:

The relativism of Einstein is strictly inverse to that of Galileo and Newton. For the latter the empirical conclusions we come to concerning duration, location and movement are relative because they believe in the existence of absolute space, time and movement.... But if their existence is believed in, all the effective conclusions we come to will be disqualified as mere appearances, values relative to the standpoint of comparison occupied by the observer. Consequently, relativism here connotes failure. The physical science of Galileo and Newton is relative in this sense.

Let us suppose that, for one reason or another, a man considers it incumbent upon him to deny the existence of those unattainable absolutes in space, time and transference. At once those concrete conclusions, which formerly appeared relative in the sinister sense of the word, being freed from comparison with the absolute, become the only conclusions that express reality. Absolute (unattainable) reality and a further reality, which is relative in comparison with the former, will not now exist. There will only be one single reality,...Relativism is not here opposed to absolutism; on the contrary, it merges with it and, so far from suggesting a failure in our knowledge, endows the latter with an absolute validity.[8]

This affirmation of the relativized perspective, of seeing an object from any of several spatial or temporal positions or from various intellectual points-of-view, becomes evident in the tendency of modern writers to renounce the single privileged view of an omniscient narrator. Faulkner's effort to see the many sides of a single story, Dos Passos' use of the many individual facets of reality, or Joyce's attempt to display the perspective of modern reality against its classical ancestry are all examples of Einstein's theory transformed into aesthetic forms.[9]

This concept of "perspectivism," as Ortega y Gasset calls it, also emphasizes the discontinuity of space and time by making us conscious of their relative status. And in doing so, it also tends to surpress causality in favor of sheer juxtaposition. One moment in time or space becomes cut off, isolated. But that single moment is now available for deeper analysis. At this point the theories of Bergson and Freud begin to act in conjunction with those of Einstein. According to Bergson, individual moments gain new depth; many new layers of memory and consciousness act simultaneously. Past and present moments permeate one another in a ceaseless turmoil. Bergson foresees the implications of this theory for the novel. Anticipating Proust's work, he stated:

> Now if some bold novelist, tearing aside the cleverly woven curtain of our conventional ego, shows us under this appearance of logic a fundamental absurdity, under this juxtaposition of simple states an infinite permeation of a thousand different impressions which have already ceased to exist the instant they are named, we commend him for having known us better than we knew ourselves. This is not the case, however, and the very fact that he spreads out our feeling in a homogeneous time, and expresses its elements by words, shows that he in his turn is only offering us its shadow: but he has arranged this shadow in such a way as to make us suspect the extraordinary and illogical nature of the object which projects it; he has made us reflect by giving outward expression to something of that contradiction, that interpretation, which is the very essence of the elements expressed.[10]

And while Bergson extended the individual moment to new depths of consciousness, Freud contributed to it a wholly new realm of impulses and motivations below or beyond the conscious.[11]

All of these developments put an increasing strain on the public currency of language itself. Could everyday words hope to function as a means of communication among beings so individually and relatively constituted? This increasing incapacity of language to convey reality is expressed on a literary level by the Austrian poet, Hugo von Hofmannsthal, in his famous 1902 "Letter of Lord Chandos." The letter explains Chandos' complete abandonment of literary activity because words have lost all meaning for him. The modes of conceptualization or of logical and absolute relationships between words or symbols and meaning are undermined. Language as heretofore used and understood no longer offers suitable forms in which the writer can cast his own experience of reality.

The modern artist, then, is faced with redefining the essential structural principles of his aesthetic work in conformity with the new scientific, philosophical, and psychological discoveries. This leads to a reconsideration of the concepts of time, space, and causality in modern art.[12] Novelists of the Twentieth

Century such as Proust and Joyce, influenced by Bergson, became interested in time experienced as a continuous flow of existence, in time as it is internally experienced rather than in clock time.

Coupled with this exploration of internal or subjective time is an exploration of internal or subjective space. There begins to appear in both painting and literature a new kind of psychic, as opposed to physical, space which, like time, flows continuously rather than being separated into discrete particles. In Futurist paintings, for example, objects merge with one another or intersect one another. Matisse's objects become at times inseparable from their background, as when the pattern on a tablecloth is not confined to the table but is continued up the wall behind it in the painting "Harmony in Red (Red Room)." Or in Expressionist painting tension is created when the psyche of the painter impinges upon and deforms the objects on his canvas in the newly created autonomous space of his picture. This new psychic space, when used in literature, provides the basis for a new type of human relationship beyond the merely visible, a kind of unity in common psychic space as experienced in many of the works of Virginia Woolf.

These two new concepts of internal time and psychic space are linked to a new concept of consciousness itself which also becomes fluid so that the present state of consciousness of an individual contains simultaneously many levels of past experience. The individual consciousness is thus greatly expanded as in some of the works of Faulkner or Döblin by a technique of spatial juxtaposition rather than chronological narration.

A wide range of intellectual innovation, then, has contributed to the exhaustion of the technique of the omniscient narrator and that of the naive use of traditional spatial and temporal sequences. The combined action of all of these cultural forces creates a pressure for artistic innovation that leads to the experimental forms we are examining.

If the modern foundations of relativity have made the omniscient narrator with his claim to absolute authority untenable for many twentieth-century writers, then the author must find an alternate way of generating coherent meaning. Structure becomes particularly important where the function of authorial guidance is no longer located in a single speaker. The elimination of a single authoritative narrator does not imply a remission of authorial control (as Wayne Booth continually stresses in his *Rhetoric of Fiction*). It is still Joyce who controls *Ulysses* and Faulkner who provides meaning in *As I Lay Dying*. The single omniscient narrator may have been "executed," as Spielhagen demanded, but the author is alive and well. The authorial control, however, has shifted; it has gone underground. The author now exerts his control not through the mouthpiece of a single character, but through the very juxtaposition of incidents, characters, and pieces of information. The author now transmits meaning through the structure of the book itself, through the interrelation of parts of each aesthetic whole.[13]

Authors have always provided meaning through structure, of course, but once the guiding voice of the omniscient narrator is removed, a greater burden is placed directly on structural organization. The meaning of the narrative work whose understanding was enhanced by commonly held traditions, values, and beliefs must, in modern works, be supported more directly from within by its own skeletal structure. Through selection and structuring the author presents his perception of order (or the lack of it) in a reality no longer tractable to absolute authority or narrative omniscience. It is not by accident that so much literary criticism of the Twentieth Century has been concerned with just this problem of narrative structure and technique.

Since the number of multilinear novels appearing in this century is so overwhelming, I have opted for a selective rather than an exhaustive study of these works. For reasons of structural variety coupled with thematic similarities, these four novels offer a particularly fruitful representative sampling. One group of multilinear novels has, however, deliberately been excluded: the postfigurative novels, those multilinear novels built upon a single, recognizable, earlier literary text, such as Joyce's *Ulysses*. These novels present a second order of structural complication since the reader must analyze them in juxtaposition to the earlier prefiguring text and its structures. The investigation of such works would form a sequel to the present study. For the moment, however, the complexities of the first order of structural innovations in the multilinear novel will present a more than ample field of investigation.

There remain, of course, a great many contemporary writers who continue to write in what we could consider the more traditional mode of straightforward narration prevalent in the Nineteenth Century. In fact, most "popular writers" of the Twentieth Century would fit into this group. I hope, however, that a close look at the innovators in narrative technique will yield insights into the direction of the novel in its entirety.

JOHN DOS PASSOS, 1924

II
John Dos Passos
Manhattan Transfer

JOHN DOS PASSOS' *Manhattan Transfer*,[1] published in 1925, represents an early example of multilinear structure in the twentieth-century novel. It not only reflects the fragmented multiple structure of other modern novels, but also displays a clear link to its immediate past, to the realistic tradition of the major nineteenth-century novels. Like many nineteenth-century novels of realism, *Manhattan Transfer* takes place in an urban environment with its constant economic and social pressures. Yet it also resembles the earlier novels in its social scope, its cast of important characters. Unlike the earlier works, however, *Manhattan Transfer* displays discrete characters whose stories do not necessarily overlap or even meet tangentially. Dickens or Balzac might introduce a large cast of varied characters, but they always depict them in reference to a single essential plot line; seemingly accidental characters like Miss Havisham or the convict in *Great Expectations* eventually prove to be intimately related to the central story of Pip's life. Dos Passos, on the other hand, feels no compulsion to create aesthetic unities among the many characters in his field of observation. Perhaps it is this very dissociation which prompts George Becker in his recent study of Dos Passos to call *Manhattan Transfer* "the full implementation of nineteenth-century realism in the American novel, though with a difference."[2] The difference lies in Dos Passos' refusal to reduce the multilinearity of his aesthetic universe to the unilinearity of the earlier novel form.

Becker goes on to describe *Manhattan Transfer* as a novel of social cross section:

> While the cross section was by no means Dos Passos' invention, with *Manhattan Transfer*...he brought it to a perfection unmatched by any of his predecessors...

> What he had before him as examples were works as various as Flaubert's *Madame Bovary* and *L'Education Sentimentale*, Zola's *L'Assommoir*, and *Pot-Bouille*, the contemporary novels of Benito Perez Galdos.... It must be noted emphatically that there was no American cross-section novel of magnitude before this work.... Certainly Dos Passos learned from his predecessors, but he did not draw slavishly from them. Rather he took the salient characteristics of this form as it had been variously developed and gave it his own unique embodiment.

> This type of novel does not have fixed rules but can be described as a kind of mosaic, or, better, a revolving stage that presents a multitude of scenes and characters which, taken together, convey a sense of the life of a given milieu and by extension give the tone of contemporary life generally. The strategy is to move the reader through a varied series of actions involving a broad and representative cast of characters. It is inductive, a sort of Gallup poll, by which the meaning is the sum of all the parts.[3]

Joseph Warren Beach refers to the same phenomenon as Collectivism in his essay "*Manhattan Transfer* Collectivism and Abstract Composition."[4]

This description of the novel implies that Dos Passos is really after a composite of the individual lives which form Manhattan, the story of the city itself where human lives are "transferred" across rivers, through time, and up and down the social scale while Manhattan itself is transferred through the early 1900's, World War I, and the immediate post-war era. As Beach points out "It [Manhattan] is the social nexus which the collectivist is seeking." But he goes on to show that this very nexus is ironically missing from Dos Passos' Manhattan:

> These people live in the same world, the same city.... But for the social nexus binding man to man—affection, gratitude, obligation, cooperation—this is nowhere to be seen.[5]

The tension in *Manhattan Transfer* is not really between the individual and the city but rather within each character; it is a struggle of each individual with himself to escape the pattern of his own isolated existence amid a plethora of other discrete existences. Manhattan provides a spatial unity within which the chaotic individual lives can interact, collide, merge, and separate over the temporal span of approximately a quarter of a century. The book's structure embodies the interaction of discrete parts and the endless repetition of themes and situations that spans them all.

I

Manhattan Transfer consists of 136 separate passages of narration and eighteen lyrical chapter introductions. At the center of those passages (passages sixty-eight and sixty-nine) are scenes embodying some of the major themes of Dos Passos' novel. Passage sixty-eight begins just after a distraught George Baldwin threatens Ellen with a pistol. The scene is a crowded restaurant in which most of the main characters of the book are assembled for the first and only time. The dialog has centered on the war as the word "Sarajevo" echoes through the room and on the Canarsie murders of an old man and a young girl. The scene closes, however, on the lone figure of Jimmy Herf walking home through Brooklyn in a thunderstorm. Jimmy reflects on the conversations of the day, on the war and anarchy and on "all the hushdope about sex" which he has just been discussing with the homosexual Tony Hunter:

> He walked on through Brooklyn. Obsession of all the beds in all the pigeonhole bedrooms, tangled sleepers twisted and strangled like the roots of potbound plants. Obsession of feet creaking on the stairs of lodging-houses, hands fumbling at door-knobs. Obsession of pounding temples and solitary bodies rigid in their beds.
>
> > J'ai fait trois fois le tour du monde
> > Vive le sang, vive le sang....
>
> Moi monsieur je suis anarchiste.... 'And three times round went our gallant ship, and three times round went our gallant ship, and three times round went'...goddam it between that and money...'and she sank to the bottom of the sea'... we're in a treadmill for fair.
>
> > J'ai fait trois fois le tour du monde
> > Dans mes voy...ages.
>
> Declaration of war...rumble of drums...beefeaters march in red after the flashing baton of a drummajor in a hat like a longhaired muff, silver knob spins flashing grump, grump, grump...in the face of revolution mondiale. Commencement of hostilities in a long parade through the empty rain-lashed streets. Extra, extra, extra. Santa Claus shoots daughter he had tried to attack. Slays Self With Shotgun...put the gun under his chin and pulled the trigger with his big toe. The stars looked down on Fredericktown. Workers of the world, unite.
>
> > Vive le sang, vive le sang.[6]

Jimmy's perception of the endless repetition of senseless existence ("we're in a treadmill for fair") is intensified as the chapter closes with the words, "Desperately he walked on."

The description of human activity as a treadmill and series of obsessions reinforces one of the book's main structural principles—repetition. Frequently the same situation will recur in a person's life or in the lives of several of the characters. Ellen's love affairs, suicides, death by fire, fire engines, ferryboats, people being struck by moving vehicles produce a continual feeling of déjà-vu as we read through the sections of the novel. Sinclair Lewis cites this fact as one of his few complaints about the book:

> Another complaint is debatable. Possibly Mr. Dos Passos returns too often to certain matters—the processes and the results of promiscuous amour, fires and fire-engines and, for a curious addition, ferry boats. (I would ask my psychoanalyst about this ferry-boat complex, but he has turned bootlegger.) However this repetition does give a sense of the repetitions of life, and the kinship of all the swirling city-crowd.[7]

The repetition is, however, not only a thematic but also a structural principle to which we will return later for a closer analysis. Each of the characters constantly retraces his own steps or those of another character; each is trapped on his own treadmill. Jimmy Herf himself will eventually complete and reverse the action begun by Bud Korpenning at the beginning of the book. Jimmy will also repeat the downward social movement of his uncle Joe Harland whose initials he shares and who appears in the passage immediately following Jimmy's ruminations in the rain.

Passage sixty-nine concerns Joe Harland, a broken-down, has-been financial wizard whose refrain is, "Things aren't always a man's fault...circumstances...er... circumstances." Harland has just been thrown out of a working-class house by an irate, weary, greyhaired mother. She screams, "I don't allow no drunken bums in my house. Git along outa here, I don't care who brought you." (p. 240). To which Harland responds in a characteristic day-dreaming retreat into the past:

> Harland looked at Joey with a little sour smile, shrugged his shoulders and went out. 'Charwoman,' he muttered as he stumbled with stiff aching legs along the dusty street of darkfaced brick houses.
> The sultry afternoon sun was like a blow on his back. Voices in his ears of maids, charwomen, cooks, stenographers, secretaries: Yes sir, Mr. Harland, Thank you sir Mr. Harland. Oh sir thank you sir so much sir Mr. Harland sir... (p. 240).

Joe Harland's waking dream is paralleled at the beginning of passage seventy by Ellen Thatcher-Oglethorpe-Herf-Baldwin's awakening from dreams. Assuming the fetal position in which she warded off the boogey-man of the night of her childhood, Ellen faces another day:

> Red buzzing in her eyelids the sunlight wakes her.... A truck jangles shatteringly along the street, the sun lays hot stripes on her back. She yawns desperately and twists herself over and lies wide awake with her hands under her head staring at the ceiling.... Ellen sits up shaking her head...but somewhere in her there lingers a

droning pang, unaccountable, something left over from last night's bitter thoughts. But she is happy and wide awake and it's early. She gets up and wanders round the room in her nightgown (p. 240).

The passages about Ellen and Joe Harland resemble one another in the negativity of their descriptive words and phrases: Harland's stiff aching legs, the dusty street, darkfaced brick, sultry afternoon sun "like a blow on his back" and Ellen's "desperate" yawn, (reminiscent of Jimmy's "desperately" walking on), the truck jangling "shatteringly," the moan of a steamboat and "a droning pang, unaccountable, something left over from last night's bitter thoughts." The two passages also share a quality of anesthetization or mesmerization by the past which causes present activity to be aimless. Joe Harland and Ellen are, then, also trapped on Jimmy Herf's treadmill. Lost in his remembrance of things past, Joe Harland stumbles along in sunlight that assaults him rather than facilitates his progress. And Ellen, unable to recall quite what it is in her past that torments her, the "something left over from last night's bitter thoughts," wanders round—an activity characteristic of her unceasing but aimless search for some kind of security and happiness.

The constant movement with no goal or guiding principles, made more difficult by interloping memories or the immediate impinging dissonance of the city itself, becomes one of the defining traits of Dos Passos' characters. Whether it is Bud Korpenning stepping off the ferry as the novel opens or Jimmy Herf stepping off the ferry as it closes, or Stan with his automobile "Dingo," or Ellen on the train at Manhattan Transfer, all the characters in the book stumble, wander, roam, stagger through the stages of their lives, their paths crossing, joining, separating in no discernable pattern. Is there, amid this chaos of motion, any unifying structural principle by which the reader can determine progress or regress? Or are we forced, in our assessment of how far the characters have come, to answer as Jimmy Herf does in the final words of the novel, "I dunno...Pretty far?" Is Jimmy Herf's debarkation at sunrise returning to the country at the novel's close any more hopeful than suicidal Bud Korpenning's debarkation into the city at its opening? Dos Passos makes us ponder over the possibility of meaning amid the mazes of individual fates that intersect and overlap to form the closely woven texture of the book. In addition, his lyrical chapter headings, which seem to tell a story of their own, force us to scrutinize more closely the overall organization of the novel.

II

The 136 narrative passages of the book are divided into eighteen distinct chapters separated into three main sections. (See diagram in the Appendix for a

visual summary of the organization of the novel.) The first five chapters forming
Section I correspond roughly to a period from the early 1900's to just before World
War I. Consisting of eight chapters, Section II corresponds approximately to the
war years. And the five chapters of Section III involve the immediate Post War
years.

In addition to chronological distinctions, the three large sections are divided by
the types of characters introduced in them. In the third section, for example, the
cast of newly introduced characters is dominated by con artists (Jake and Rosie
Silverman and Jack Cunningham), lower-class people forced into a life of crime by
the desperation of the depression (Dutch Robertson and his girl, Francie), and
those who rise to social prominence by dubious activities (Nevada Jones and
Congo). The two notable exceptions are the laborers Anna Cohen and her friend
Elmer, who are forced into labor strikes by poor working conditions. Theatrical
people dominate the second section—Ruth, Cassie, Jojo Oglethorpe, Goldweiser,
and Tony Hunter. Only Stan Emery, whose real vocation seems to be drinking and
driving his car, is not directly involved in the theater except through his interest in
Ellen. Joe O'Keefe also stands outside the theatrical circle although his per-
formances as a labor organizer who informs to big business almost qualifies him
for the stage.

The first section presents the most heterogeneous group of characters—
ranging from the down-and-outers Bud Korpenning and Joe Harland to business
and professional men Jeff Merivale, Phineas P. Blackhead, Mr. Emery, George
Baldwin, and Phil Sandbourne. The accountant Ed Thatcher and his family, Mme.
Rigaud, and Gus and Nellie McNiel fall in between these two extremes on the
social scale. The one common denominator among these characters seems to be
their level of aspiration. Ed Thatcher dreams continually of the big money he will
make for his daughter while Ellen herself dreams of being Elaine of Lammermoor
or the lily maid of Astalot. Emile dreams of becoming an upright small business-
man by marrying Mme. Rigaud. George Baldwin aspires to further his law career
by cashing in on Gus McNiel's dreams while Phil Sandbourne contemplates
skyscrapers. Phineas P. Blackhead is busy building his future multi-million dollar
business. Even those already at the top of the social ladder—the Merivales and
Herfs—discuss future prospects. All of these characters dwell upon future success
and aspire to later happiness and wealth. Only Bud Korpenning and Joe Harland
fail to participate in this general tropism toward higher social status. These two
characters also have dreams but they represent the past, not the future. Bud's and
Joe's lives have stagnated in memories of past errors or glories. Significantly, the
lives of these two produce the least sensation of the movement of time. While
other characters engage in a whirlwind of activities, Bud and Joe relive a single
recurring attempt to survive and escape their present condition.

The character of Bud Korpenning presents, perhaps, the most puzzling questions in the novel regarding his function. Alien to the city, Bud brings his bit of personal misery out of the country with him, hoping to drown it in his future big-city wealth. What he finds as he disembarks, however, is that Manhattan abounds in bulls, derby-hatted detectives, and callousness. His dream, to "come to New York City an git rich," fades in the pangs of his continually empty stomach. For Bud, alone of all the characters, time virtually stands still. In the barbershop scene very near the beginning of the book (pp. 16-17), Bud mentions that he is twenty-five years old. Over one hundred pages later, immediately before his suicide (p. 122), Bud again states that he is twenty-five years old. Bud does not advance in age at all while in the same one hundred pages, Ellen ages eighteen years. Why? The fact that Bud's consciousness is arrested in that one violent moment of his patricide freezes time itself in reference to Bud. Even external space becomes meaningless as Bud wanders toward his end thinking, "Don't matter where I go, can't go nowhere now.... Don't matter where I go, can't go nowhere now.... Can't go nowhere now" (p. 125). The only escape Bud finds lies in annihilating through death both time and space which trap him endlessly in the consciousness of his guilt. Amid the bustling lives and dreams and activities of the city, Bud ends the inescapable isolation of his existence by leaping into Manhattan's East River.

That may explain why time seems to stand still in Bud's lonely life, but it does not explain his role in the novel as a whole nor does it explain why he is so prominently featured in the first section which ends with his death and begins with the ferry from which he disembarks. After all, his life does not arise out of the city as do those of the other characters. His story, nonetheless, represents a distilled form of the basic dilemma confronting the city's characters—the inability to break out of self-involved isolation to establish a meaningful and lasting social connection on the vast stage of the metropolis. Each of the characters remains essentially isolated in his or her own fantasies, vices, and obsessions. Their lives may touch or overlap, but it is always the temporary conjunction of discrete, self-involved existences. That is the underlying tragedy of the novel as a whole which surfaces most forcefully in the story of Bud Korpenning.

III

One factor that lends some unity to the isolated individual lives in the book is the repetition of situations and images across the stories of different characters, across time and space, and across the 404 pages of the novel's first edition. Bud's vision of the fiery sun reflected in Manhattan's windows as he jumps to his death, for example, is echoed later in the book in Stan Emery's fatal self-immolation and Anna Cohen's near fatal burns.

Stan's story, like Bud's and Anna's, is limited to the section in which he is introduced. Again like Bud and Anna, he first appears in the second scene of the section and, like Bud, destroys himself very near its end. Stan, Bud, and Anna also represent the thematic center of gravity of their respective sections. Their problems are symptomatic of the problems central to the lives of the other characters. Stan, for example, closely resembles Jimmy Herf in his high social status and wealthy background. And, like Jimmy, he can find no activity to engage his talents. He only knows, as Jimmy does, what does *not* satisfy him. Stan's death, as his life, is without point, a fact which parallels Jimmy's lament at not having the romantic soul or the tragic sensitivity necessary to commit a dramatically forceful suicide that makes a definite statement.

And yet Stan represents for Ellen the one possibility for true emotional attachment, a possibility destroyed by his senseless death. The recurrent image of the fire engine and fire often functions in conjunction with Stan or Ellen's feelings about him. A major scene between Stan and Ellen takes place in the final passage of the chapter entitled "Fire Engine" where Stan, for the first (and last) time, openly and emotionally confess his love for Ellen, who realizes his sincerity. A moment later they see a fire engine with "Siren throbbing in an upward shriek that burst and trailed in a dull wail down the street, a fire engine went by red and gleaming, then a hook-and-ladder with bell clanging" (p. 216). The next time we meet Stan, he is married to "Pearline." The love dream is shattered, but the fire engine and the fire of passion and love that Ellen feels have become emblematic of Stan.

This association is crucial to an understanding of the closing scene of the novel's central section. It plays in a doctor's office in which a young woman prepares to have an abortion. She is never identified by name and critics are divided as to whether she is, in fact, Ellen who is pregnant with Stan's child. Her declaration to Jimmy Herf of her intention to raise Stan's baby after Stan's death appears to throw doubt on this woman in the doctor's office being Ellen—especially since Dos Passos often introduces vignettes of unknown characters who never appear again. But the woman's situation is identical to Ellen's. She is young and recently divorced and, therefore, has decided on an abortion. Ellen, too, has just finalized her divorce from Jojo. But, more importantly, prior to the scene in the doctor's office, she has started to recover from the impact of Stan's death. Larry has just proposed to her and would like to whisk her off to South America. This scene takes place aboard a ferry (another recurring image, as Lewis pointed out). At its close Ellen declares, "After all day it's exciting isn't it Larry, getting back into the center of things" (p. 267). Ellen has succeeded in returning from her mourning for Stan to the frenetic social life of Manhattan.

On the basis of external evidence, then, the young woman at the end of Section II could be Ellen. But the decisive detail depends on the reader's associating fire and fire engines with Stan—with his love and his death. After the abortion the young woman is signalling a taxi to take her to her next social engagement when a fire engine passes: "A fire engine roars past, a hosewagon with sweatyfaced men pulling on rubber coats, a clanging hook-and-ladder." The description is reminiscent of the fire engine Stan wanted to follow earlier and of the fire engines which must eventually follow him. The young woman's reaction to the moment in which the fire engine passes is rather strong:

> All the feeling in her fades with the dizzy fade of the siren. A wooden Indian, painted, with a hand raised at the streetcorner.
> 'Taxi!'
> 'Yes ma'am.'
> 'Drive to the Ritz' (p. 268).

The reaction must be Ellen's. She has just removed from her life the last real contact with Stan, the last remnant of her one true love, in order to return to the social life of the city; the passing fire engine brings the impact and the irreversibility of that gesture home to her. This scene completes Stan's own death scene; it removes him entirely from the novel. It closes Section II with the same finality with which Bud's suicide closes Section I.

Stan's actual death scene is also rather remarkable in that it ties all the chapters of the first two sections of the novel together in a single Gordian knot. The tangled skein of Stan's own life forms a center for the other tangled existences of the book. His death takes place in the chapter entitled "Rollercoaster," the shortest chapter of the novel and the only one entirely dedicated to a single character. All three scenes of the six-page chapter really center on Stan; his new wife, Pearline, occupies the last passage but is seen only in her attachment to Stan.

In the chapter's first scene, Stan, like Bud entering New York and like Ellen immediately before her abortion, finds himself on a ferryboat, a setting which recalls the first chapter heading of the book, "Ferryslip." In fact, the book's opening is not merely alluded to here but quoted verbatim. The "three gulls" which open the first lyrical passage of the novel (p. 3) appear again as Stan stands on the ferry's deck to signal an extended direct quotation in the next paragraph. The three gulls:

> wheeled above broken boxes, spoiled cabbageheads, orangerinds heaving slowly between the splintered plank walls, the green spumed under the round bow as the ferry skidding on the tide, gulped the broken water, crashed, slid, settled slowly into the slip. Handwinches whirled with jingle of chains, gates folded upward. Stan stepped across the crack, staggered up the manuresmelling wooden tunnel of the ferryhouse... (pp. 251-52).

The only differences between this passage and the opening lyrical passage of Chapter One, "Ferryslip," are a shift in tense from the present of the opening passage to past here and a shift in focus from anonymous and plural "men and women" and "feet" to Stan himself. What was a general condition of the city in an eternal and anonymous present in the opening passage becomes an individualized and personal moment in the life of a single character as Stan emerges from the ferry. What we see, then, is not just a vague recurrence of a similar event in the lives of two characters, but an almost verbatim repetition of a situation. Two scenes, separated by 250 pages, twenty-two years and social upheavals on the scale of World War I, remain identical. The city itself provides a constant, enduring through time and space and external change, in the isolated lives of two individual characters who never meet. The essential personal tragedies of isolated self-involvement within the metropolis remain unaffected by external change. Dos Passos' focus is indeed society, but it is a society formed of discrete existences physically held together by the city.

The passage quoted above is not the only direct reference to earlier chapters which appears in the "Rollercoaster" chapter. Several earlier scenes are either quoted directly or strongly alluded to. In the paragraph following that just quoted, these lines appear:

> There was Babylon and Nineveh, they were built of brick. Athens was goldmarble columns. Rome was held up on broad arches of rubble. In Constantinople the minarets flame like great candles round the Golden Horn.... Steel glass, tile, concrete will be the materials of the skyscrapers. Crammed on the narrow island the million-windowed buildings will jut, glittering pyramid on pyramid, white cloudsheads piled above a thunderstorm... (p. 252).

These sentences are a reproduction in its entirety of the lyrical passage which opens the novel's second chapter, "Metropolis." The novel's third chapter, "Dollars," is also echoed in Stan's perception. The title itself is evoked in the tune Stan recalls: "Fortynine dollars ahangin on the wall." And phrases from the lyrical introduction to the chapter recur in the description of Stan's ferry ride.

> The ferry passed close to *a tubby steamer that rode at anchor listing* toward Stan so that he could see all the decks. An Ellis Island tug was alongside. *A stale smell came from* the decks packed with upturned *faces* like a load of melons (p. 251).

The italicized phrases, though somewhat displaced in their order, are exact repetitions of phrases in the introductory passage to Chapter Three. The introductory passage to Chapter Four, "Tracks," in which a stranger finally enters the city to inquire, "Is this New York?" is also evoked in Stan's refrain, "Where am I? City of New York, County of New York, State of New York..." Even the final chapter of Section I, "Steamroller," is echoed by the title "Rollercoaster" and its lyrical introduction bears a similarity of rhetorical style to Stan's description of the city:

> Across the zinc water the tall walls, the birch-like cluster of downtown buildings shimmered up the rosy morning like a sound of horns through a chocolate-brown haze. As the boat drew near the buildings densened to a granite mountain split with knifecut canyons (p. 251).

In the very short chapter concerning Stan's death, then, each of the introductory passages to chapters in Section I is quoted, echoed, or recalled in some way. The last moments of Stan's life recapitulate the entire first section of the novel. What were lyrical passages used by the narrator to introduce chapters, to set scene and mood of the various episodes, become an actual part of the narrative itself. The narrator's perceptive imagination becomes the physical reality of his character's life—and death. The narrator is, in a sense, dispersed into the consciousness of his various characters.

But why is Stan the focus of this fusion and recapitulation? Primarily because Stan is the hope for Ellen's happiness and love, the unused potential that parallels Jimmy Herf, the heir to Bud Korpenning's self-destruction, and the father of the aborted hopes of future change. Stan represents the empty center of the novel. Of all the characters, he alone has the potential to realign the lives around him. His life is, therefore, the greatest failure of the book. He fails not only for himself, but also for Ellen, for his child, for those he might have affected positively. His is the greatest betrayal of potential and human talent. His death scene recapitulates the entire first section dominated by Bud Korpenning's death scene. But it goes beyond that to include the entire second section of the book as well.

In his whiskey-saturated consciousness, Stan recalls bits of songs, refrains and song titles. Among them are the phrases: "There's one more river to Jordan" (p. 251), "a great lady on a white horse" (p. 253), "Longlegged Jack of the Isthmus" (p. 252), "Two by two the elephant and the kangaroo" (p. 249), and "The big baboon by the light of the moon is combing his Auburn hair" (p. 250). These phrases are direct references to the titles of Chapters Eight, One, Two, and Five respectively (the last two phrases both recall the title "Went to the Animal Fair" of Chapter Five). In addition, the title of Chapter Four of the second section, "Fire Engine," is graphically evoked as Stan's wife returns to find her home and her husband ablaze. This chapter is also mentioned directly as Stan looks out through the window of his apartment at a passing fire engine (p. 252). The chapter title of Stan's death scene, "Rollercoaster," also recalls the lyrical introduction to Chapter Six immediately preceding it, "Five Statutory Questions," which begins with the description of a rollercoaster ride. Only Chapter Three, "Nine Days Wonder," is conspicuous by its absence from any direct reference in Stan's death scene. This chapter, however, prepares the stage for that death scene and its results. It is in Chapter Three that Stan establishes the fire engine as his emblem by suggesting he paint his beloved auto, Dingo, "red like a fire engine." Here, too, as Ellen's deepest thoughts run to Stan, "in deep pitblackness inside [her] something clangs like a fire engine" (p. 182). Jimmy Herf's actual introduction to Ellen occurs in this same chapter—a meeting arranged by Stan who leaves Ellen and Jimmy alone together as he will leave them permanently through his death. But more importantly, in this chapter Stan announces his highest aspiration—to fail. "Why the hell does everybody want to succeed? I'd like to meet somebody who wanted to fail. That's the only sublime thing" (p. 175). Failure, total self-destruction, is the one goal Stan will, ironically, succeed in reaching.

The chapter of Stan's death, then, not only recapitulates all of Section I, but also ties all the chapters of Section II together into a tight, tangled knot. When Bud Korpenning commits suicide as "the windows of Manhattan have caught fire" at the end of Section I, he destroys only his own isolated torments. When Stan Emery goes up in the blaze he has set toward the end of Section II, he takes all the hopes and aspirations of the first two sections with him. Destruction and waste have moved from a single life to involve many lives.

This theme of growing destruction and waste becomes even more prominent in Section III of the novel as Anna Cohen follows in the footsteps of Bud and Stan. Like her two predecessors, Anna is introduced in the second scene of her section. Like them she will face destruction amid flames in an accidental fire reminiscent of the fire of Stan's death and the fiery windows of Manhattan as Bud jumps from the bridge to his death. Anna's near fatal accident will also be immediately preceded by a dream closely resembling Bud Korpenning's dream at his death scene.

During his suicide, Bud had envisioned himself riding in triumph through New York with his new bride. He pictures himself as the center of adulation in the city which had heretofore taken no note of him at all. He imagines that he and his bride are fabulously wealthy, respected, and successful in the urban world. As the flames of her dressmaking material begin to engulf her, Anna, too, foresees a triumphal ride through New York with her new husband Elmer. She sees Elmer as Valentino, the perfect lover, who is also feted as one of the city's most valued members during a procession similar to that in Bud's dream. These dreams which surround tragic destruction share two basic components—the desire for personal fulfillment in love and marriage and the desire for social and economic success. One or the other of those two components represents the primary driving force in the lives of each of the characters in the book. Those two dreams, coming in the first and last sections of the novel, bracket the smaller dreams and failures of all the other characters. When these dreams literally "go up in flames," the reader is left very little about which he can be optimistic.

Anna's and Bud's dreams also serve as a background and foil for Stan Emery's scene of destruction. Stan's death chapter is placed symmetrically between the chapters of Bud's and Anna's destruction. ("Rollercoaster" is separated by six intervening chapters from the "Steamroller" chapter of Bud's death and "The Burthen of Nineveh" chapter in which Anna is badly burned. See the narrative matrix in the Appendix for verification.) Stan's death represents the inverse of the other two destruction scenes. In Stan's life, Bud's and Anna's dreams are already fulfilled. Stan has economic security and social prominence and he has also just acquired a new wife—the major components of the other dreams. However, the fulfillment of the dream has not produced any satisfying meaning in Stan's life. He is, apparently, unhappy with his new wife: "He shot headlong through the open door and down the long hall shouting Pearline [his wife's name] into the livingroom. It smelled funny, Pearline's smell, to hell with it" (p. 252). Likewise, economic security, money, becomes fuel for Stan's death pyre as he thinks, "A thousand dollar fire, a hundred-thousand dollar fire, a million dollar fire. Skyscrapers go up like flames, in flames, flames" (p. 255). This last sentence is particularly ominous since Stan's last articulated wish on the preceding page was "Kerist I wish I was a skyscraper." Apparently, then, even the outward fulfillment of the novel's most essential dream cannot save the characters from meaningless self-destruction.

Anna's near fatal accident in Section III not only echoes Bud's and Stan's stories in Sections I and II, but also echoes the fates of other characters in the last section of the book. The destruction of Dutch Robertson and his girl Francie, of Jake and Rosie Silverman, and of Phineas P. Blackhead and his partner Densch occur in this final section. The destruction that began with the isolated character, Bud Korpenning, in Section I and spread by Stan's indirect associations in Section II becomes an unavoidable physical reality in Section III as a number of characters face physical, financial, and emotional ruin.

IV

The third section introduces a complicating theme in its study of human destruction—that of victimization. In this section the theme of characters preying on one another economically and psychologically, which has been implicit in the earlier sections in the stories of George Baldwin, Emile, Joe O'Keefe, and others, gains major importance. Not only are poor characters like Dutch and Francie forced to prey upon the rich through robbery, but also the very rich characters like

Jack Cunningham and James Merivale prey on one another to accrue even greater wealth and social advantage. Big business continually exploits workers like Anna and Elmer as political rhetoric swells to workers' slogans. One of the more subtle forms of exploitation takes place on the personal level, however—the exploitation by Ellen of Jimmy Herf and his son Martin.

After Stan's death, Ellen and Jimmy go off to Europe to help as volunteers in World War I. They marry and return with a son, Martin. As Ellen becomes re-established among her social circle in New York, she no longer feels the need for the emotional security Jimmy provides. She separates from him and eventually divorces him to marry George Baldwin. Ellen discards Jimmy as another toy she has outgrown and with about as much regard for his feelings. Ellen returns to the self-centered life characteristic of her since childhood.

But physically Ellen has moved from childhood to motherhood. In doing so, she · comes to repeat the devouring self-interest of her own mother, "poor Susie." Ellen conveys to her child, Martin, the same insensitivity her mother displayed toward her. She abandons Martin to the fearful shadows of the night just as her mother abandoned her in a traumatic childhood experience. The two scenes are similar. In both Ellen's and Martin's childhood experience the feelings of abandonment by the mother and the resulting isolation are intensified by the darkness and shadows which seem animated and threatening to the small child. Both Ellen and Martin respond to the black emptiness by shrieking to fend off the chaotic noises of the city outside their bedrooms. Ellen's change of roles from child to mother, from victim to victimizer, merely recreates the feeling of abandonment rather than altering it through personal experience. This repetition of the childhood trauma in Sections I and III represents another case of the pessimistic outlook built into the structure of Dos Passos' novel. The repeated scene even gains in negativity as Martin is burdened not only with a fear of the dark, but also with an inherited recoil from the fire engine and the spoiled love and failed hopes it has come to represent. The basic patterns of human life remain the same, then, through all three sections of the novel. The raw materials of human experience—the fears and dreams and hopes and disappointments—recur from generation to generation. The cycles of individual lives repeat in endless dreary succession.

V

It is important to note that the city, Manhattan itself, has a fate of its own, turning it into a character of the book much like the human characters. Its story is told, primarily, in the lyrical section headings used to introduce each chapter of the novel. In those lyrical passages, the city becomes a living organism or, rather, an animated machine which shuttles people about "like apples fed down a chute into a press" (p. 3). Every aspect of the city becomes animated as:

> Night crushes bright milk out of the arclights, squeezes the sullen blocks until they drip red, yellow, green into streets resounding with feet. All the asphalt oozes light. Light spurts from lettering on roofs, mills dizzily among wheels, stains rolling tons of sky (p. 112, "Steamroller").

The urban animation here is of a particularly oppressive and violent kind. The city is a massive, impersonal press where the archetypal forces of darkness (night) and light (here pointedly artificial) vie with one another in gestures of pressure expressed by words such as "crushes," "squeezes," "oozes," "spurts." From the very beginning of the novel, then, the city is a setting of intense impersonal force into which each human individual drops. Night, as the "Steamroller," closes Section I and "Morning clatters with the first L train down Allen Street" (p. 129) to open Section II. In these lyrical passages, the city has its life cycle of days and nights, winters and springs just as individual human characters do. It, too, experiences a cyclical repetition.

But the long life of the city also allows it to encompass historical repetition, the prediction of its own possible doom. In the lyrical introduction to Chapter Two, Section I, "Metropolis," Manhattan is aligned with the greatest cities in history:

> There was Babylon and Nineveh; they were built of brick. Athens was gold marble columns. Rome was held up on broad arches of rubble. In Constantinople the minarets flame like great candles round the Golden Horn.... Steel, glass, tile, concrete will be the materials of the skyscrapers. Crammed on the narrow island the million-windowed buildings will jut glittering, pyramid on pyramid like the white cloudhead above a thunderstorm (p. 12).

But this passage is ambiguous. It places New York among the ranks of the greatest cities, but it also places her among cities doomed to destruction. This same optimistic passage from Section I takes on an ominous tinge as it is repeated verbatim in Stan's death scene in Section II. The passage is alluded to in even more negative terms by the self-proclaimed tramp-prophet "Jonah" in Section III. In a discussion with the Angel Gabriel and two frightened young boys, the tramp examines the city's future and concludes that, in contrast to the cities of Babylon and Nineveh, God will need a mere seven seconds to destroy the sinful "old bitch" Manhattan. Jonah suggests that what the city needs is earthquake insurance against divine wrath. The reference to the city as the "old bitch" calls up the Whore of Babylon image employed in the Bible and by Döblin in *Berlin Alexanderplatz*. According to this prophet, divine retribution will be visited upon New York—"an Brooklyn an the Bronx" along with it. He goes on to explain how the end is near, and how just yesterday he persuaded the Angel Gabriel to refrain from "foreclosing" on the city for a week or two. Eventually, however, Jonah predicts that the primal elements of fire, earth, and water will reunite to spell oblivion for the city and return the world to its primitive state as he says, "But it's terrible to think of, folks, the fire an brimstone an the earthquake an the tidal wave an the tall buildings crashing together" (p. 381).

This passage, however, serves more to temper than to reinforce the first prediction of doom. Playing on the earlier idea of Earthquake Insurance, the tramp uses the terminology of big business and the slang of the city itself implying that Manhattan would have to commit a kind of metropolitan suicide which would be difficult to imagine. The passage is, furthermore, spoken by a character of dubious mental competence. The two young boys who are listening eventually retreat from the madman to "the regularly spaced safe arclights and the street" of the city itself for what the children see as protection. But what tempers the passage most is the similarity of its final phrase, "the tall buildings crashing together," to the lyrical passage which begins this final chapter "The Burthen of Nineveh." The physical violence and animation of that phrase is evident here also:

> Seeping in red twilight out of the Gulf Stream fog, throbbing brassthroat that howls through the stiff-fingered streets, prying open glazed eyes of skyscrapers, splashing red lead on the girdered thighs of five bridges, teasing caterwauling tugboats into heat under the toppling smoketrees of the harbor.
>
> Spring puckering our mouths, spring giving us gooseflesh grows gigantic out of the droning of sirens, crashes with enormous scaring din through the halted traffic, between attentive frozen tiptoe blocks (p. 371).

But the violence of this passage is one of regeneration not destruction, of rebirth not of death. Spring generates this violence. The city survives despite the destruction and waste of the individual lives within it. It possesses a generative violence that grinds continuing endurance and life out of inanimate structures. The city survives on its own raw vitality and momentum. It is largely indifferent to the human lives within its bounds. It collects and contains them in physical space; it intrudes upon their isolation with its noise and power; it witnesses their births and deaths—and it endures. It is the native environment for the characters who thrive on its frenetic activity—for Ellen and George Baldwin, for Gus McNiel and Congo, for the Merivales and Jack Cunningham. And it is the hell which swallows Bud and Anna and Stan in flames and from which the more sensitive and idealistic Jimmy Herf must escape.

VI

Jimmy Herf's final escape from the city, an escape he has desired during most of the novel, actually resembles a return from the mouth of hell:

> Out of the empty dark fog of the river, the ferryslip yawns all of a sudden, a black mouth with a throat of light. Herf hurries through cavernous gloom and out to a fogblurred street. At the top of a hill he stops to look back. He can see nothing but fog spaced with a file of blurred arclights (pp. 403-04).

In his escape, Jimmy brings the action of the novel and the life of the city to a close in one final repetition. Just like Bud in the novel's opening, Stan before his death, and Ellen before her abortion, Jimmy Herf finds himself standing on a ferry. This time, however, the ferry is carrying him away from the city rather than into it.

Surrounded by flowers and spring, Jimmy finally leaves the city. He is the only character who does so. This may indeed seem like a positive gesture by Dos Passos, salvation through flight. Jimmy is, indeed, engulfed in a "morning pearliness" and sunrise as he explores the countryside. But he also finds himself "walking along a cement road between dumping grounds full of smoking rubbishpiles." The smell is noxious; Jimmy is hungry, and his feet are blistered. He spends his last quarter on food in the country as Bud had done when he first entered the city. He encounters a "redhaired man" in a truck as Bud had met a "redhaired man" behind a lunch counter. But Jimmy is even more disoriented than Bud who had at least set out to get "to the center of things" (p. 4) in the city. When asked how far he is going, Jimmy can only respond, "I dunno...Pretty far."

The similarities in Bud's escape into the city and Jimmy's out of it tend to negate any very optimistic reading of the novel's end.[8] It reads, rather, as another inevitable repetition of human activity. The city certainly intensifies the pressures of modern existence, as its image as a "press" and the opening passages quoted earlier demonstrate. But it is not the city that destroys the individuals within it; it is the inescapable repetition of failure and desperation. The ineluctable repetition itself becomes the primary structuring principle of the novel. Dos Passos does present a bleak view of urban life, but his critique is more sweeping. Jimmy's escape from the concentrated pressures of the city do not, finally, deliver him from hell. The country provides its own demonic, red-haired characters as well as its own lack of guidance or salvation. Jimmy's flight from the city only serves to change the setting of his desperation. The city contains all the stories of Dos Passos' novel in physical and temporal proximity so that we can see dreams and delusions transferred from one character to another in Manhattan. Its animation creates an additional pressure in life which concentrates the dilemmas of modern man so as to make them more readily observable, but the city alone is not the creator of those difficulties. Jimmy's flight to the country does not promise to be any more successful than Bud's flight from it. Modern man carries his existential crises of statistical determinism and individual responsibility within him. Dos Passos chooses the city of Manhattan as the most appropriate means to make those crises painfully and most intensely visible.

VII

The dominant structural principle in Dos Passos' *Manhattan Transfer*, then, is repetition. A study of the book's structure with reference to a narrative matrix has helped to reveal the extraordinary exactness of the physical positioning and the thematic content of that repetition. It is not the incremental repetition of a single sacrifice scene, as we will see in the life of Franz Biberkopf in *Berlin Alexanderplatz*. Nor is it the repetition of an overriding mythic pattern that plays itself out at the expense of individual consciousness, as we will see in Faulkner's *As I Lay Dying*. It is, rather, the repetition of basic human situations, of individual loves and hopes and failures and deaths, in which all the many characters of the book participate. The recurrences here are on a smaller scale than those of Faulkner's novel and are less personal than those of Döblin's book. Dos Passos' novel could almost be seen as a study of the human life-cycle with Manhattan as an animated catalyst. This view of the book recalls the realistic ancestry of the text and corresponds closely to the suggestion of Becker and Beach that Dos Passos' work is the culmination of the nineteenth-century realistic tradition in the novel and the beginning of its revision. Dos Passos is not so deeply interested in the consciousness of any one of his characters as he is in their social behavior, in their observable life patterns. Unlike Faulkner who reveals a struggle of human consciousness against the larger forces of existence, Dos Passos depicts the struggle of the individual against his own inevitable life-cycle and the environment which nurtures it.

In one way, the outlook of *Manhattan Transfer* is almost naturalistically bleak.[9] No one wins; no one escapes; and no one dies heroically. Even the struggle itself lacks the dramatic force of the struggles of Franz Biberkopf or the Bundren Family. Manhattan reveals a more crass economic and psychological struggle beneath or beyond which the narrator cannot see. It is a critique of a very unpointed variety, of human existence in general. Its structure is essentially simpler than the philosophical profundity of Faulkner's work and the technical ingenuity of Döblin's novel. *Manhattan Transfer* does, however, manage to evoke a social scope unattained in either of the other works. The novel does, in a way, represent the Gallup Poll approach which Becker suggested. But it is a significant poll. It reveals that social status, social upheaval and change, historical progression are insignificant factors in the life cycle of an individual human organism. Senseless death, failure, and disillusionment override all external factors of social position or historical period. To this end *Manhattan Transfer* is more oppressively pessimistic than either Döblin's or Faulkner's novels. Here even the drama and glory of the human struggle are obscured by its inevitable sameness through the lives of many individuals. Psychologically and emotionally isolated but biologically and socially trapped in the mass of humanity, Dos Passos' characters resemble the existential heroes of a much later period and different culture.

The multilinearity of the book reinforces the basic thematic concerns of Dos Passos' *Manhattan Transfer*. This structure buttresses the meaningless and fragmented complexity of modern urban existence where primal leitmotifs, such as fire and the related color red as well as fire engines, water or the crossing of it, darkness and light, and the larger repetitions of human existence, births, deaths and suicides, marriages, provide not a hopeful unity but rather an ineluctable reiteration of desperation. Separated by the self-involved quality of their own consciousness, the characters live out discrete plot lines which fail to meld into a larger unity of meaning as the earlier nineteenth-century novels had often done. *Manhattan Transfer* represents a basic pattern of simple multilinearity providing a model that was modified and complicated by later authors.

ALFRED DÖBLIN, 1929

III
Alfred Döblin
Berlin Alexanderplatz

BY ENTITLING HIS novel *Berlin Alexanderplatz* (1929), Döblin acknowledges his debt to Dos Passos' *Manhattan Transfer*; he clearly envisions himself within the tradition Dos Passos represents. Döblin's novel resembles Dos Passos' not only in its title but also in its depiction of big city life, the metropolis and its effect on the individual. *Berlin Alexanderplatz*, however, is really closer in structure and technique to Dos Passos' *USA* trilogy which was not published until 1938, almost a decade after *Berlin Alexanderplatz*.

In contrast to the multilinearity of plot in *Manhattan Transfer*, the structuring elements of *Berlin Alexanderplatz* are far more diverse and complex, and its surface even more apparently chaotic. The full title of the work might lead one to expect a basically two-part focus; although Döblin originally entitled his book only "Berlin Alexanderplatz," the addition (at the request of his publisher) of the subtitle "Die Geschichte vom Franz Biberkopf" underlines one of the major conflicts of the work and creates an immediate duality between the social collective of the city and the story of an individual. It further suggests an implicit tension between the fate and identity of the named individual and the anonymous, impersonal speed and mobility of a city as conveyed in the name of one of its street car stops. This basic tension of the individual's struggle to reconcile himself to the flux and confusion of modern urban existence will remain one of the major themes and generators of new perceptions throughout the work. Berlin not only provides a background and setting for Franz's story, but also becomes a character in its own right.[1] The depiction of the collective life of Berlin, the interpolated narrations of the lives of unnamed individual citizens, the physical procession of speed and mechanical power is constantly juxtaposed to Franz's own attempts to become an upstanding member of that urban community. Immediately after we are introduced to the newly released prisoner, Franz Biberkopf, in Book I, we meet his main adversary, Berlin itself, in Book II. Indeed, the beginning of the second book is devoted largely to establishing the spatial, human, and temporal dimensions of the collective entity, Berlin. The duality of the title does not, however, adequately reflect the complexity of the novel as a whole. If we were to attempt to force this novel into a two-dimensional matrix of the sort sufficient for *Manhattan Transfer*, we would have to expunge precisely those details, digressions and diversions which create its structure, which support the larger thematic concerns of the book. The real structuring elements of this novel are not twofold but manifold.

I

Franz Biberkopf, a furniture mover and cement worker, is a rather simple, physically strong, lower-class character. He becomes involved in some unspecified way with the Berlin underworld, particularly with his friend Herbert and his mistress Eve, who was Franz's former mistress. Franz's great strength and short temper eventually get him into difficulty when he beats his second mistress, Ida, causing fatal internal injuries. For this act, Franz is sentenced to four years in Tegel prison. The novel opens in the fall of 1927 as the thirty-year-old Franz is thrust out of the confining but protective walls of Tegel and is forced to face the city of Berlin.

Despite his former troubles, good-hearted and naive Franz sets out to become an upstanding citizen. But he is drawn again into the underworld life of the city, where he is betrayed by his "friend" Lüders, involved unwittingly and involuntarily in a robbery in which he loses his arm, and finally loses his new love, Mieze. As a result of his trials, Franz nearly succumbs to insanity when he is mistakenly arrested for Mieze's murder. Eventually he recovers, reborn as a new, emotionally and psychologically stronger character who has learned to survive and thrive in the city.

Franz's limited education and mental capacity and his low social status would not lead us to expect the rhetorical polish of extended biblical and literary allusions or the scope of historical consciousness which permeate the book. The reader is left to puzzle over how this simple criminal from the slums of Berlin fits into a network of allusions to Jeremiah and the *Oresteia*. This kind of apparent disparity in the text leads the reader to question the function of the allusive material as well as of the political and historical documentation in the story of this extremely limited consciousness, Franz Biberkopf. To determine whether the techniques of the novel are truly at odds with its plot or whether there are structural principles which hold these disparate elements together in a coherent unity, the reader is forced to scrutinize the structure of the novel more closely.

II

Even the earliest critical readers of *Berlin Alexanderplatz* had no difficulty in identifying its structural complexity and aligning it with works such as Joyce's *Ulysses*. In a review in "Leipziger Neueste Nachrichten" December 11, 1929, E. Kurt Fischer commented:

> Der Kampf um die neue Romanform geht weiter. Fast alle Romanschriftsteller von Rang haben sich in den letzten Jahren abgewendet von der Form der gleichmässig fortlaufenden Erzählung, in der der Autor seine Ansicht von den Dingen, sein Bild der Welt in einen erlebten oder erdachten Vorgang hineinprojiziert.[2]

> The battle for a new form for the novel continues. Almost all novelists of note have, in recent years, turned away from the form of the uniformly unfolding story in which the author projects his view of things, his picture of the world in the form of experienced or invented incidents.

Efraim Frisch focuses more closely on the proximity of Döblin's work to other structural experiments in his comments in the *Frankfurter Zeitung* of December 29, 1919:

> Es liegt nahe, an Joyce zu denken, die gleiche sprachliche Dichtigkeit, das Assoziative, ineinandergearbeitete, durch Wortzeichen wie Blinkfeuer den dunklen Knäuel des Unbewußten belichtend, das Rhapsodische, der rasche Wechsel der Formen.[3]

> It reminds one of Joyce—the same linguistic density, the associative, interwoven, illuminating like lightening the dark coil of the unconscious through catchwords, the rhapsodical, the rapid change of forms.

However, few critics have attempted to analyze the structural complexities of *Berlin Alexanderplatz* in any detail. As with Faulkner's *As I Lay Dying*, the lack of a single, coherent, reliable narrator places an additional burden of meaning on the form of the work. Juxtaposition, sequence and repetition of related images must convey the novel's meaning. Most critics have acknowledged that structure is indeed important in the work, but they have contented themselves with identifying the form as a reification of the chaos and complexity of the city.[4] Although this is undoubtedly one of the effects of the book's structure, we must ask if there are not also more consistent patterns of imagery and allusion that create a coherent unity of meaning amidst the chaos of the urban setting.

Theodore Ziolkowski has taken a major step in the investigation of this problem when he observes the triadic pattern of classical drama embedded in the texture of the novel. Ziolkowski proposes that the novel obtains its unity of action and its basic rhythm by a "conscious travesty of tragedy with all its most characteristic elements."[5] He analyzes the details of the three main setbacks in Franz's attempt to be "anständig": Lüders' deception, the loss of his arm and, finally, the loss of Mieze. After drawing supporting material from Döblin's radio play version of Biberkopf's story, Ziolkowski concludes:

> The preliminary statement of the narrator can now be read as an argumentum preceding the tragic action. The main action consists of a series of three reversals of fortune precipitated by the hero's Hamartia, that is, by his blindness with regard to human nature and his boastfulness.... This action is accompanied, finally, by a chorus of voices that reflect on the meaning of Biberkopf's destiny and that see far more clearly than he the greater implications of all he does and experiences. The final shift from romantic belief in fate to a modern awareness of reality is a kind of catharsis, precipitated by a series of scenes that make artistic sense only if they are viewed as a pursuit by the Erinyes....[6]

Ziolkowski's suggestion regarding the Erinyes is particularly interesting if we recall that the furies at the end of *Oresteia* join forces with Athena to promote the welfare of the newly arising *city* of Athens, to insure the successful union of the collectivity; the irrational fates bend to the rational persuasion of men as a society. Similarly, Berlin as a collective is preserved in Döblin's work. As Ziolkowski points out, the image of the city in the novel shifts from the threatening Whore of Babylon to the beneficial collective; its powers now promote Franz's incorporation into a union with other men. Ziolkowski also offers an analysis of the manner in which this travesty helps to determine the rhythm and structure of the novel:

> If we arrange the nine books of the novel according to this threefold rhythm, a definite pattern emerges. Book 1, which records Biberkopf's release from prison and his first efforts to regain his equilibrium..., is really only an upbeat to the first principal episode. The three main episodes then dispose themselves into pairs of books (2 and 3, 4 and 5, 6 and 7), each of which shows the same rhythm, but with increasing intensity. The first book of each pair depicts Biberkopf's recovery from the preceding blow, while the second builds up to the next blow, which comes regularly at the end of Books 3, 5, and 7. Books 8 and 9 together constitute another group, inasmuch as they depict his recovery from the blow at the end of the seventh book and the turning point, his arrival at the completely new view....[7]

Going beyond this persuasive analysis of one overall pattern, however, one could scrutinize more closely the patterns created by individual strains of allusion and documentation. Several strains are immediately evident: biblical and literary allusion; documentary materials such as medical texts, popular songs, legal decrees, news clippings; and interpolated narratives. While some critics claim that these elements serve only to interrupt and loosen the main plot line of the novel in the interest of a kind of chaos of realism, I would argue that they, on the contrary, generate meaningful patterns of their own which complement or compete with the basic organizing features which Ziolkowski has pointed out.

III

A series of biblical allusions permeating the work is the most prominent among the interpolated strains of outside material. Several critics have gone so far as to list the biblical references[8] and Helmut Schwimmer in his book *Alfred Döblin: Berlin Alexanderplatz* provides a helpful analysis of the way in which particular quotations work in the specific contexts in which they appear. But I have discovered no attempt to follow the allusions through the entire work to investigate their coherence.

If we pursue the biblical references through the novel, we do, indeed, discover a coherent pattern of allusions that firmly buttresses and parallels the structure which Ziolkowski suggests in his analysis of the classical tragedy components. The biblical references, too, form a triad of temptations and trials dividing the book roughly into the same segments which Ziolkowski proposes. These three steps are represented as three main trials of biblical legend—the temptation of Adam and Eve in the Garden, the tribulations of Job, and the sacrifice of Isaac by Abraham. These three main allusions form an incremental repetition of the theme of sacrifice and victims.

Adam and Eve in the Garden represent the temptation of naive innocence which overestimates its own capacity to deal with knowledge and power. Their fall is caused partly by pride and partly by a naive inability to recognize evil, the dirt and grit which is inevitably mixed with one's "Butterbrot." This initial fall of innocence parallels and reinforces Franz's own first fall, when he discovers he has been deceived and betrayed by Lüders. Franz's naive boastfulness and overestimation of his own capacity to control the situation unite with the harsh, degraded reality of the lower classes of urban humanity to bring about Franz's temporary undoing.

The references to Adam and Eve begin in Book II and are developed largely in Books II and III, thus paralleling the first division in Ziolkowski's analysis of Franz's three trials. There is, however, also a carry-over of the image to Book IV where the narrator comments on the inevitability of temptation in the world and also on the human weakness upon which it preys (p. 131).[9] The immediate context of this comment is the corruption of the solid middle-class Gerner couple by their naive hopes for easy money. The comment further underlines the inescapable nature of temptation in a real world and its destructive effect on those who naively succumb to it.

The second main biblical reference is to the story of Job, another story of the trials of an innocent man. This time, however, naiveté no longer appears as a component. Job's difficulty lies not in his inability to recognize evil, but rather in his desire to defeat it by his own strength. Döblin's Job is a willful man who regrets above all else the loss of his own strength and power. His pride, although battered, is far from dead. His pride and over-estimation of his own strength keep him from humbly accepting a divine cure. "Die Stimme" warns Job that he does not want to be cured; he is still too willful.

This second temptation occupies largely the fourth and fifth books of the novel, again paralleling and reinforcing Ziolkowski's second main structural division and providing an interpretive parallel to Franz's second trial. Upon recovering from his first blow by Lüders, Franz finally reenters life in Berlin with his over-confidence in his own physical strength still undaunted. He refuses to understand that his individual strength is not equal to the challenges of urban reality. Over-estimating his ability to deal with Reinhold and his gang, Franz is again crushed by external reality. Like the physically weakened and diseased Job, Franz too becomes physically weakened when he loses the symbol of his brute strength, his arm. And like Job, Franz will have his night of wrestling with "Die Stimme," which becomes the voice of death, in his own purification and rebirth at the asylum at Buch.

The third major biblical story (contained largely in Books VI and VII, and corresponding to Ziolkowski's third major division) is that of the sacrifice of Isaac by Abraham. Again Döblin employs a trial by temptation to help explain Franz's third tribulation, the loss of Mieze. This final story in the series adds one more feature to the loss of naive innocence in Adam and Eve, and the destructive force of individual willfulness, pride, and dependence on personal strength in Job. In order for Abraham's sacrifice to be a redeeming act, Isaac must willingly consent to be the victim. He must come to see and accept the need for his own destruction. Franz, too, must come to see and understand his own guilt and inadequacy; he must become a willing victim, a self-sacrificer, as Mieze has become. Franz's instinctive return at this point to Tegel, the scene of his earlier punishment for personal guilt, is perhaps a sub-conscious recognition of the need to accept personal responsibility for his deeds and the guilt which that responsibility generates. Franz begins here to acknowledge the need to become a willing victim. Only when Franz can utter "Ich bin schuldig" in his night of delirium at Buch will he be truly reborn.

The three biblical stories taken together, then, form an incremental repetition of the basic theme of temptation and tribulation and its effect. Franz, like Adam and Eve, must relinquish his naiveté; like Job, he must realize the inadequacy of his personal strength and wish to be cured; and finally, like Isaac, Franz must become a willing victim, accepting personal responsibility and guilt. These three episodes, paralleling what Ziolkowski sees as the rhythm of Greek tragedy in the novel, reflect and help to explain Franz's own trials.

Biblical allusions also serve one other structural function. Three other major groups of references from Jeremiah, from Ecclesiastes, and from Revelations separate or punctuate these three main stories. These references serve not only as a frame for the biblical stories discussed above, but also as an editorial tool to aid in the interpretation of both the biblical stories and Franz's own story.

The first of these references comes from Jeremiah. While the old Jew looks at Franz in Book I, he thinks, "Sprach Jeremia, wir wollen Babylon heilen, aber es ließ sich nicht heilen.... Das Schwert komme über die Kaldäer, über die Bewohner Babylons" (p. 14). ("Thus spoke Jeremiah, 'We wanted to heal Babylon, but it would not let itself be healed.... Let the sword come over the Caldeans, over the inhabitants of Babylon'.") This is the earliest mention of Babylon, which then becomes a recurrent image in the second half of the novel. Significantly, the old Jew is not regarding Berlin and its evils here, but is rather focusing on Franz himself, on his recalcitrant refusal to be helped. The usual association of Babylon (and particularly the image of the Whore of Babylon) with the decadence and decaying urban life of Rome cannot be so easily transferred to Berlin. The Whore must represent, at least, Franz's own attitude toward the city which is his adversary—or perhaps even Franz's attitude in general, his overbearing pride and self-confidence that he can maintain control, can rule in any situation.

The image of Babylon, now specifically the Whore of Babylon, recurs in Book VI. The gilded facade and alluring richness of the Whore is juxtaposed to Franz's own temptation to make easy money by becoming a petty thief and fence and to his remembrance of killing Ida and his consequent drinking problems. Again the allusions here to the Whore of Babylon focus more on temptations within Franz's own psyche than on those of Berlin as a modern "imperial city." It is important, too, that at the beginning of Book VI, at the beginning of Franz's last trial (his loss of Mieze), the reference shifts from Jeremiah's prophecies of destruction to an image from the Book of Revelations, an image immediately adjacent to the birth of a new world. The Whore of Babylon, then, represents a pivotal image, a turning from destruction and retribution to rebirth through purgation. This shift is particularly striking coming from Döblin, who at this time was becoming engrossed in his Judaic heritage. That he should draw this single image from the New Testament cannot have been an accident. It represents, rather, a conscious turning away from destruction and toward regeneration within the biblical images.

The Whore of Babylon reappears in Book VIII in an unavoidable confrontation with Franz who must now come to terms with the reality of Mieze's death and his own responsibility and guilt. Franz's final confrontation with the Whore comes in his moments of delirium at Buch. Franz must now face and purge the false pride and personal deterioration he has experienced in Berlin's underworld. In a struggle for Franz's mind, the Whore combats Death. Death, however, wins out. The old Franz is sacrificed on the same altar upon which the Whore herself is consumed. Now able to face and accept his guilt, Franz is reborn as a new man, a new part of the collectivity of Berlin.

The image of Babylon from Jeremiah and Revelations brackets the central stories of Adam and Eve, Job, and Abraham and Isaac. They form a framework within which the specific steps of Franz's temptations are worked out, and they supply imagistic support for that progression.

In Franz's final moment of purification before his rebirth at Buch, he utters the words, "Ich bin schuldig. Ich bin ein Vieh" ("I am guilty. I am a beast."). With this acceptance of his own guilt, Franz brings about his redemption. He also brings full circle the last major group of biblical references—those from Ecclesiastes. Franz's line "Ich bin ein Vieh" recalls an earlier statement in Book IV, "Denn es geht dem Menschen wie dem Vieh" ("For it is with men as with dumb beasts."). This line introduces the slaughter-house descriptions reminiscent of Gottfried Benn's Morgue Poems. These descriptions of the slaughter of helpless dumb animals in a modern, clinically accurate way lend dramatic impact to Franz's second trial, the loss of his arm, in Books IV and V. Franz's unconscious repetition of this image at Buch, his acceptance of his role of sacrificial victim, tempers and completes these earlier references.

Another phrase from Ecclesiastes provides a constant refrain in Books VII, VIII, and IX: "Ein Jegliches hat seine Zeit." To every thing there is a season, and a time to every purpose under heaven.... The time that is approaching in Book VII is Mieze's. The time of her death is fulfilled in a progressive intensification—to the point of expressionistic incoherency—as night and the storm unite with Mieze's fear and suffering to produce the climax of her death at the end of Book VII. The time is also that of Franz's approaching purification and rebirth as the phrase again appears in Book VIII and finally merges into Death's dialog with the Whore of Babylon in Book IX, when Death declares, "Es ist Zeit...." The two strains of Ecclesiastes and Revelations finally unite here. Franz sends the seeds of his being back to nature and God to be reborn, another reference to Ecclesiastes (11:6).

In a novel which outlines the progress of a man from naive arrogance and willful pride to the acceptance of his role as sacrificial victim and his rebirth into the community of men, Ecclesiastes seems a particularly appropriate biblical reference. Beginning with the sentiment "Vanity of vanities; all is vanity,"

Ecclesiastes bears directly on Franz's problems and development. Even Franz's final salvation through incorporation into the community, an ending which has seemed so contrived to many critics and troublesome even to Döblin himself,[10] receives a certain logic based upon repeated imagery in its echoing of Ecclesiastes 4:9-12:

> Two are better than one; because they have
> a good reward for their labour.
>
> For if they fall, the one will lift up
> his fellow; but woe to him that is alone
> when he falleth; for he hath not another to
> help him up.
>
> Again, if two lie together, they have heat:
> but how can one be warm alone?
>
> And if one prevail against him, two shall
> withstand him; and a threefold cord is
> not quickly broken.

Shortly before Franz's triumphant march with the masses, he thinks:

> Viel Unglück kommt davon, wenn man allein geht. Wenn mehrere sind, ist es schon anders. Man muß sich gewöhnen, auf andere zu hören, denn was andere sagen, geht mich auch an. Da merke ich, wer ich bin und was ich mir vornehmen kann....
> Er ist Hilfsportier in einer Fabrik. Was ist denn das Schicksal? Eins ist stärker als ich. Wenn wir zwei sind, ist es schon schwerer, stärker zu sein als ich. Wenn wir zehn sind, noch schwerer. Und wenn wir tausend sind und eine Million, dann ist es ganz schwer.
> Aber es ist auch schöner und besser, mit andern zu sein (p. 409).

> Much unhappiness comes from one's marching alone. Whenever there are several, it is different. One must accustom himself to listening to others, because what others say also concerns me. Through this I recognize who I am and what I can undertake.
> He is an assistant porter in a factory. What is fate? One is stronger than I am. If we are two, it is more difficult to be stronger than I am. If we are ten, still more difficult. And if we are thousands or a million, then it is indeed difficult. But it is also nicer and better to be with others.

Although the rhetoric is also that of the communist propagandists, the biblical parallels provide a more coherent (if less politically forceful) interpretation. This final affirmation of community and of personal responsibility within the community brings Franz's progress full circle while completing also the circle of biblical references that have provided order, meaning, and structure for that chaotic development.

The biblical passages, then, are more than accidental evocations of Holy
Scripture for dramatic effect. They are, also, a structuring force providing a framework and an interpretive tool for the main points in Franz's life story. They form
an incremental repetition of trials and temptations in the stories of Adam and Eve,
Job, and Abraham and Isaac. And each of these, in turn, is introduced by a biblical
admonition. The Adam and Eve story is preceded by Jeremiah's comment on
Babylon's recalcitrance; Job's dilemma is anticipated by the Ecclesiastes passage
which equates the plight of men and animals; and the Abraham and Isaac tale is
prefaced by Jeremiah's warning not to trust in the flesh alone and by the
appearance of the Whore of Babylon herself from Revelations. Ecclesiastes and
Revelations join in the final books as the Whore is defeated, injustice acknowledged, and personal responsibility within the community accepted. These references provide a kind of logic of imagery which supports Ziolkowski's reading of
the rhythm of the novel and provides some justification, at least on the level of
imagery, for its problematic ending.

IV

To determine whether the novel's other manifold montage elements work in
the same way as the biblical allusions, buttressing an irresistible central pattern, or
whether they interfere with this main movement, we must examine those components more closely.

Let us turn first to the literary allusions in the novel. As Helmut Schwimmer
points out in his book *Alfred Döblin: Berlin Alexanderplatz* (pp. 105-08), minor
literary allusions abound in one-line references and puns, but there is also a group
of sustained allusions which punctuate the novel at crucial points. These fall
roughly into the following categories: those from classical Greek literature, those
from German romantic literature, and finally those which reflect modern dramatic
literature within the "drama" staged in Franz's asylum room at Buch.

One of the earliest sustained references is to Kleist's *Prinz Friedrich von
Homburg*. It occurs in Book II when Lina flings the homosexual newspaper back at
Weisskopf as Franz watches with amused pleasure. The narrator comments:

> Im Kriegsgebiet machte Lina, die herzige, schlampige, kleine, ungewaschene,
> verweinte, einen selbständigen Vorstoß a la Prinz von Homburg: Mein edler Oheim
> Friedrich von der Mark! Natalie! Laß, laß! O Gott der Welt, jetzt ists um ihn
> geschehn, gleichviel, gleichviel! Sie rannte spornstracks, schnurstreichs auf den
> Stand des Weisskopfs (p. 64).

> On the field of battle Lina, the dear, messy, small, unwashed, teary-eyed Lina made
> an independent assault a la Prinz von Homburg: My noble Uncle Friedrich von der

Mark! Natalie! Let be, let be! O God in heaven, now he's lost, no matter, no matter! She ran with all possible speed straight for the stand of Weisskopf.

The reference here to Kleist's passionately patriotic work has a mock heroic effect in the context of a battle between a prostitute and a pornography peddlar. There is real human feeling and heroism of a sort in Lina's action, but the narrator exploits rather its comic absurdity.

This same mock heroic quality, the deflation of a truly passionate and elevated literary work by its juxtaposition with degraded modern reality, is picked up again a short time later in Döblin's references to Aeschylus' *Oresteia*.[11] The murder of Agamemnon and the tragic retribution which it demands is juxtaposed to Franz's murder of Ida, for which only four years at Tegel makes amends. Orestes' being pursued by the Furies is juxtaposed to Franz's undisturbed mundane existence. The narrator coyly asks:

> Hetzen ihn, von früher her, Ida und so weiter, Gewissensbedenken, Albdrücken, unruhiger Schlaf, Qualen, Erinnyen aus der Zeit unserer Urgroßmütter? Nicht zu machen. Man bedenke die veränderte Situation (p. 84).

> Is he tormented from days gone by—Ida and so forth—by pangs of conscience, nightmares, restless sleep, agonies, Erinyes from the time of our great-grand-mother? Not a bit. One must consider the altered circumstances.

The answer, of course, is that they do not torment him. Modern physics can explain Ida's death; it requires no mythic foundation. Telegraphs and telephones have replaced the beacon fires of Greece; modern functionality replaces Greek tragic fervor.

Besides its mock heroic aspect, however, this juxtaposition of Greek tragedy and modern prosaic functionality has a more subtle effect. It is a deflating instrument for some of the narrator's and Franz's own rhetoric about "Schicksal," about dramatic and uncounterable blows from the outside which threaten to crush "our hero," Franz Biberkopf. Here in Book II, prior to Franz's first "blow by fate," the narrator signals to the reader that his own earlier rhetoric in the introduction to the entire novel must be taken with a grain (or perhaps a sack) of salt. The narrator explains in the introduction that Franz wants to be decent and that he succeeds in the beginning. However, although things are going tolerably well economically, he becomes entangled in a regular battle with something that comes from outside, that is unfathomable and that looks like a fate (p. 7). Even here the narrator is careful to write, "looks like a fate." That is, it looks like fate to Franz in his naive state of irresponsibility early in the book.

Another classical reference occurs in Book IV, this time from Homer's *Odyssey*. The passage recounts Menelaos' stories to Telemachus which recall Odysseus' past glories and spur Telemachus to return to his homeland. Franz at this point struggles to return too, from his own stupor after his betrayal by Lüders. Franz, too, seeks to recover a lost life. But the classical passage rapidly deteriorates into a stream-of-consciousness association by the narrator on the quality of various types of chickens! The effect is, of course, humorous in a Shandian way. It is also reminiscent of the workings of Franz's own mind which returns so often to his stomach and its needs. But again, the effect is one of deflation of rhetoric and sentiment. The glory that was Greece is not really comparable to the "Brathühner" that are Berlin.

The allusions to Greek classics, then, work ironically against reading Franz's story as though it were a Greek tragedy. They continuously deflate the idea of "Schicksal," of fate in the Greek sense, in a world of modern, functional reality. When Franz finally comes to be a part of the collectivity that is Berlin, he comes home to a community of working, marching men, not to a divinely nurtured *polis* under Athena's protection. These references, therefore, are consistent with Ziolkowski's contention that Franz moves away from a Greek view of fate and toward a modern view of urban reality.

There is, however, one intermediate step in his progress, and it is marked by literary references to the German romantic collection of folk songs of Achim von Arnim and Clemens Brentano, *Des Knaben Wunderhorn*. The poem entitled "Erntelied. Katholisches Kirchenlied" supplies what will become a refrain in the second half of the novel. The poem, as it appears in the novel, runs:

> Es ist ein Schnitter, der heißt Tod,
> hat Gewalt vom großen Gott.
> Heut wetzt er das Messer,
> Es schneidt schon viel besser,
> Bald wird er drein schneiden,
> Wir müssen's nur leiden,
> Hüt dich blau Blümlein.

> There is a reaper, who's called death,
> Who has his power from the great Lord.
> Today he sharpens the knife,
> It already cuts much better,
> Soon he will cut away,
> We can only endure it,
> Be on your guard, little blue flower.

This text first appears in Book V as Franz begins to think that he has had enough of Reinhold's girl-swapping. Franz's decision to teach Reinhold a lesson will, in fact, precipitate the loss of Franz's arm and Mieze's death. This motif of "der Schnitter, Tod" appears again in Book VI as Franz lies in the hospital recuperating from the amputation of his arm. It reminds the reader that it was Franz's arrogant attempt to reform Reinhold that put him there; it recalls Franz's personal responsibility for this second apparently "fateful" blow. The refrain again occurs as Franz recovers his personal pride and arrogance while finding a room (p. 214). It reappears when Franz boasts to the anarchist in a pub that he doesn't work, but has others work for him (p. 242). For Franz, then, the refrain signals his arrogance and its destructive consequences throughout his life.

The particular phrase, "there is a reaper," also occurs in reference to Mieze. In Book VII when Mieze first goes for a walk in the woods with Reinhold, the refrain sounds its ominous note. The episode occurs shortly after the interpolated story of the murder of Pussi Uhl by her lover who, significantly, changed his name to von Arnim. The motif is intensified later in Book VII when Reinhold murders Mieze. Violence builds to near-frenzy as nature combines with literary references in a romantic pathos at Mieze's death, "Gewalt, Gewalt, ist Schnitter, vom höchsten Gott hat er die Gewalt." "Power, power, is a reaper, from the mighty Lord he has the power" (p. 317).

The emphasis again shifts to Franz and his personal realizations as he learns of Mieze's death in Book VIII:

> Und er denkt an Miezeken, da steigt etwas auf, eine Angst steigt auf, ein Schrecken winkt herüber, es ist da, ist ein Schnitter, heißt Tod, er kommt gegangen mit Beilen und Stangen, er bläst ein Flötchen, dann nimmt er die Posaune, wird er die Posaune blasen, wird er die Pauken schlagen, wird der schwarze furchtbare Sturmbock kommen, wumm, immer sachte, rumm (p. 345).

> And he thinks of little Mieze, then something arises, a fear arises, a terror beckons to him, it is here, the reaper, named death, he is coming with axes and poles, he blows a small flute, then he takes the trumpet, he will blow the trumpet, he will beat the drums, the black, terrifying battering ram will come, vroom, ever more slowly, vroom.

The passage not only looks back to Mieze's death and Franz's boastful and arrogant attempt to toy with Reinhold, but also looks forward to Franz's night of self-confrontation at Buch and to his rebirth. This "reaper" motif appears again after Franz is reborn in Book IX (p. 402). It is, perhaps, a warning for Franz not to fall into the same errors of his previously romantic outlook and also a conclusion to that part of Franz's life where he himself was the frail and naive "little blue flower." The refrain appears for a final time during Franz's testimony at Reinhold's trial. The romantic image is now, however, coupled with Franz's realization of his own responsibility for Mieze's death:

Dann sackt er auch schwer in sich zusammen und hält sich die Hand vor die Stirn. Es ist ein Schnitter, der heißt Tod, ich bin deine, lieblich ist sie zu dir gekommen, hat dich beschützt, und du, Schande, schrei Schande (pp. 409-09).

Then he sank heavily into himself and held his hand to his forehead. There is a reaper, who's called death, I am yours, lovingly she came to you, protected you, and you, Shame, cry Shame.

As with Greek references, this romantic reference also works ironically against its own literal statement. While speaking of unavoidable, fateful death, it continuously recalls Franz's personal guilt and responsibility for his own lost arm and Mieze's lost life. It brings Franz a step further from the Greek view of fate and a step closer to modern reality with its insistence on personal responsibility.

The last literary reference is not really an allusion to any specific work but rather the incorporation of a literary technique from modern drama or the dream play. In the asylum at Buch Franz reviews his life and development in the theater of his own mind. With the continual repetition of the phrase "Herankommen lassen," he confronts at once all the montage elements of Berlin, its people and streets and songs, and he reviews his setbacks and his personal guilt. This procession of the theater of his life finally triggers Franz's repentance. In reexperiencing his life, Franz finally achieves the epiphany that allows him to relinquish his former self, to die symbolically and be reborn as a new man with a modern view of reality and of community and of personal responsibility. And, finally, the literary references have come into line with their own effect. Unlike the ironic use of the Greek and Romantic references cited earlier, this technique from modern drama does, in fact, make Franz realize the nature of modern reality's emphasis on individual responsibility.

As with the biblical allusions and the rhythm of Greek tragedy, we again see a three-part movement in the literary references from an ironic use of Greek classicism to an ironic use of German romanticism and finally to the use of a technique of modern drama. These references, however, do not fall into the neat two-book pairs of the first two elements. Rather, they divide the novel roughly into three sections. The early books of Franz's naive view of fate give way in Book V to the romantic refrain and finally, in Book IX, to a more modern insistence on the responsibility of the individual in the face of an impersonal urban reality. The literary references, then, parallel the three-beat rhythm of the biblical allusions and structures of Greek tragedy. They reinforce the three-step progression of Franz's coming to understand his own position in the tragedies of his life. But at the same time, they complicate the physical structure of the novel by reflecting the time lapse between the events of the plot and Franz's realization of their meaning.

V

The literary references, then, provide a complicating factor; they overlay and obscure the central plot pattern at the same time as they reinforce the basic triadic rhythm of the novel. The remaining structural components provide even further complications which contribute to the richness of the book's meaning and to its difficulty as well. These added elements give the book its somewhat syncopated surface rhythm and its reputation as reified chaos. The structural components which contribute to this syncopation are the use of documentary materials, ranging from weather reports to official documents to medical texts, and the use of interpolated narratives.

Unlike the structuring techniques discussed so far, none of these factors functions to reinforce the triadic progression we have noted to this point. They seem, rather, to have a single sustained function as a class and also specific local functions in individual contexts.

The interpolated narratives, for example, seem to maintain a dominant function throughout the entire novel—namely, to illustrate the conflict between the individual personality, the individual identity, and the demands, expectations, or conventions of society at large. The technique thus echoes the basic dichotomy of individual versus society that we noted earlier in examining the title of Döblin's novel.

Before we examine the use of this technique in particular contexts, let me explain specifically what I mean by "interpolated narratives." As the term implies, interpolated narratives refer to relatively sustained stories intruding upon the main plot line of Franz's own development. These stories generally refer to a character not central to the Biberkopf plot development or to characters who have been removed from that central plot (e.g., Mieze's own story late in the novel in Book VIII after she has died). This would indicate that the interpolated narratives act as retarding forces, slowing the flow of the main plot. They do, however, echo and amplify the general stages of Franz's development, contributing allusively to the flow of physical action. There may be some overlap of these stories with what I will call documentary material, since some of the interpolated narratives may, in fact, concern real, historically verifiable persons. The interpolated narratives are usually self-contained units, however, which appear at only one point in the novel although they may be extended over several pages as with the stories of Zannowich and Bornemann. Most of the documentary material such as weather reports and quotations from text books or ads recur throughout the novel.

Turning now to the individual interpolated narratives, we can explore their immediate functions as well as the overall pattern which they create in the course of the book as a whole. The earliest, and one of the most extended, interpolated narratives occurs in Book I in a section headed "Belehrung durch das Beispiel des

Zannowich." The red-headed Jew is attempting to teach the newly released
prisoner Franz Biberkopf by telling him a story in the biblical tradition of parables.
Significantly, of all the interpolated narratives, only this one and its sequel are told
directly to Franz. All the others are provided by the narrator for the reader's
benefit. This gives the Zannowich story a somewhat privileged status. Its use as a
tool in Franz's education serves as a paradigm for the reader in his own reaction to
later interjected stories. And that same model reflects also the intent and effect of
the novel as a whole. As the narrator states in his introduction to the entire book:

> Dies zu betrachten und zu hören wird sich für viele lohnen, die wie Franz Biberkopf
> in einer Menschenhaut wohnen und denen es passiert wie diesem Franz Biberkopf,
> nämlich vom Leben mehr zu verlangen als das Butterbrot (p. 7).

> To contemplate and to listen to this story will be useful to many who, like Biberkopf,
> live in a human skin and who attempt, like Franz Biberkopf, to demand more from
> life than their bread and butter.

The narrator echoes these introductory lines very near the end of the novel, after
Franz has been reborn and returns to a new life in Berlin (p. 406). The telling of
Franz Biberkopf's story, then, has a deliberate and strong didactic impulse which is
reflected in the "Belehrung durch das Beispiel des Zannowich." The Zannowich
story, in turn, provides a model for the reading of the remaining interpolated
narratives.

The Zannowich story is, basically, that of a man whose identity is at odds with
his social environment. Because society can more easily accept him as a nobleman
than a peasant, he changes from Zannowich to Baron Warta. Then, inspired by his
easy deception, he becomes the descendant of a famous folk hero, Prinz von
Skanderbegs, and borrows money he is unable to return. Zannowich is eventually
unmasked and thrown into prison where he commits suicide at the age of thirty—
precisely Franz's age as he is released from prison. Franz, who had been enjoying
the triumphs of personal ingenuity over a duped society, reacts with heated
sympathy to Zannowich's undoing. Society, he surmises, has been unfair to a poor
sinner. Franz, of course, identifies with Zannowich: he, too, will adopt an attitude
of personal accomplishment and self-reliance in opposition to rather than in
conjunction with his own social context. And like Zannowich's, Franz's attempt to
assert his own identity by his own ingenuity will end in near suicide. The false-
identity theme of the Zannowich story will be repeated later in the Bornemann
story in Book VII but with the story's main thrust reversed. Bornemann is trying
not to conquer and profit from the society he is deceiving, but rather to escape
from it entirely.

Like both Franz and Zannowich, Bornemann has served time in prison. He, however, escapes and in doing so encounters a corpse with whom he exchanges identities and becomes a fish dealer named Finke. He lives peacefully until his stepdaughter recognizes and denounces him. Finke is compared explicitly to Franz, but ironically it is just at this point that Franz is most forcefully trying to reassert his personal identity. He convinces the Pums Gang to take him in by asserting that if Franz Biberkopf says he is "in on the deal," they had better believe it. And when Reinhold consents to visit him, Franz feels his personal control return as he attempts to project a self-confident image by reasserting his identity as Franz Biberkopf. Franz, however, finally loses his identity, too, in his furious attack on Mieze as the concealed Reinhold watches. As Franz loses his temper, he also loses his name, the symbol of his personal identity, as evidenced in his stream-of-consciousness during the attack: "Der Franz Biberkopf aber, —Biberkopf, Lieberkopf, Zieberkopf, keinen Namen hat der—" (p. 301). The actual deterioration in Franz's proper name represents the deterioration of his control and his attempt to maintain a personal identity. Franz, as his identity is slipping, comes to resemble Bornemann. But whereas Franz's loss of identity is not a conscious act, his attempt to project a forceful and controlled identity is. It is that self-confident, self-sufficient facade which Reinhold will force Franz to relinquish, as Finke is forced to relinquish his identity.

In a more complex way than the interpolated stories examined earlier, the Bornemann story, like the Zannowich story, parallels Franz's own. It is not, however, a story told to Franz; rather, it is told by the narrator to the reader to help elucidate Franz's development. It is yet another story of a false personal identity in conflict with and finally unmasked by society. The attempt of the murderer Beese to become Von Arnim in the Pussi Uhl Story again reflects this same theme with the same result.

In a formal sense, the story of Pussi Uhl belongs to the second major category of interpolated stories—i.e., those which depict the disappointment or destruction of an individual's personality through social interaction. The story strangely parallels those of both Franz and Mieze. Labelled by the narrator as a "Schicksalstragödie," the tale relates how a flyer is shot down, cheated out of his inheritance, how he slips into a life of crime, changes his identity several times, serves a prison term, eventually kills the prostitute with whom he lives, and ends in a state of mental collapse. The narrator takes a rather cynical view of the whole story, thus undermining his description of it as a "tragedy of fate." The fate of Pussi herself resembles that of both Ida, Franz's murdered lover, and Mieze who will be murdered in the next book.

But Beese, unlike the male characters discussed earlier, is duped by society rather than deceiving it himself. He is cheated, disgraced, and eventually ruined by his interaction with an aggressively dishonest society. Döblin presents several such characters whose lives are either harmed or destroyed in negative social interactions. In Book II, in a tavern scene, Döblin momentarily observes several such pieces of human wreckage. One young man has recently been fired from his position for speaking honestly, another is a dope addict whose short term in the army led to the insane asylum, another is a young girl used by an older, wealthy man. The depiction of such tainted lives reaches a point of high intensity in Book III as a war veteran loses his ailing child because of the doctor's failure to come to his aid. The story of the Gerner couple's temptation by the desire for easy money through burglary in Book IV also fits into this category, as does that of the young couple in Book V who commit suicide because of economic problems, and the carpenter and his deformed family in Book VI. In Book VII several characters come into legal conflict with their society: a chauffeur and housemaid, as well as the flyer Beese, and Bornemann/Finke. The depiction of these legal difficulties gives way to that of a girl disappointed in her boyfriend and, finally, to that of a suicidal young woman disappointed with life in general.

The first seven books of the novel, then, contain interpolated narratives of individual people in a variety of conflicts with society. Some of the stories demonstrate the folly of attempting to foist a false, personally defined identity on society, while others reveal the minor tragedies of lives spoiled by social inter-actions.

The main interpolated narrative in Book VIII is Mieze's life story. She is now dead, and having been removed from the action, she becomes no more than a statistic, depersonalized and incorporated into a larger social record (p. 341). Mieze's tragic death is reduced to a mere technical process; the length of a human life becomes compared to a length of telephone wire (p. 341). The valuing of human life which holds society together as an organic whole gives way here to a technological sense which makes society an artificial construct. Society takes no note of personal identity and suffering; it must depersonalize, lump, and classify into useful categories. The narrator recounts Mieze's story in a very factual and unemotional manner, as he did the earlier stories about strangers. He then, however, breaks into a very emotional investigation as to the justice of Mieze's death, lamenting that her love for Franz and her mere proximity to him leads Mieze to her death. The narrator ends his comments with "that's life" (p. 340-41). The idea of fate, "that's life," and coincidence is implicit here, but so also is a sense of personal responsibility. Mieze dies because of her association with Franz. Franz and not society is indicted for Mieze's murder. "Sie wurde zerschlagen, weil sie dastand, zufällig neben dem Mann..." (p. 341). Even amid impersonal social forces, human beings retain a degree of personal responsibility—a fact which Franz must come to recognize.

Mieze's story, too, is told by the narrator to the reader. Its impersonal and matter-of-fact style generalizes her personal fate by making her one more individual whose life is destroyed in the city. But, since the reader already knows Mieze personally, her story also has the effect of drawing all the other interpolated narratives into a more sympathetic and personal sphere. But Mieze's story produces a dichotomy of feeling in the reader. We value her social relationship to Franz and Eva, but it is precisely that which kills her. Döblin values interpersonal, social contact, but he also realizes its potentially destructive force for the individual—"because such is life." Perhaps this realization is what made Döblin wince at his own ending. The interpolated narratives running through the entire novel darkly shadow whatever optimism Döblin may feel about social community. They produce a constant dissonance, contradicting the rhythmic three-step progress of Franz's life.

The final interpolated narrative in Book IX, as does the preceding Mieze story, expresses Döblin's dilemma. He sincerely wants to affirm the communal and social potential of the urban setting. But he also knows the destructive power inherent in human relationships when these are complicated by the crushing dehumanized forces of modern society. The story of the mother and her seven sons who refuse to renounce the God and heritage of their people, the cultural treasures of their society, and so suffer a triumphantly heroic death is inspiring but disturbing. Is the price of maintaining a society the sacrifice of many of its best individual lives? The interpolated narratives keep that question in the reader's and narrator's minds and make Döblin's final affirmation of society extremely problematic. The biblical tone of this last story extends the question to all of human history and makes its solutions more philosophically pressing.

These interjected stories, then, complicate one of the novel's main themes, that of the individual's responsibility to his society. They also provide a structural complication since they are scattered throughout the entire book in no discernible pattern. They tend to obscure the central triadic rhythm of Franz's development.

VI

Another complicating factor is the use of documentary material. It includes such disparate items as weather reports, accounts of the Tunney-Dempsey fight, and of the Prague earthquake, quotations from medical texts on impotence and digestion, popular songs, discussions on varieties of chickens and on the age of the sun. These references serve mainly to keep a kind of cosmic background alive in the reader's mind, to provide a perspective from which to view Franz's individual development. The great natural forces of weather and earthquakes, the great social forces of war and history, and the great urban forces of the day-to-day functioning of a large city run relentlessly through the book as Franz stumbles, falls, and begins his personal journey again. On the one hand, the wealth of backgrounding tends to dwarf Franz's story. The irresistible forces of life roll on despite his setbacks. But, on the other hand, the use of documentary material draws Franz's own story into those great forces, generalizes and universalizes it. Döblin even uses some of his documentary techniques in Franz's story, frequently providing exact dates the way a writer of a war report or news article would.

The documentary material itself provides a kind of continuous dissonance, a collage of natural, historical and social forces, rather than any coherent pattern. It is the chorus of Berlin, Germany and the world, recurrent notes of a universe larger than Franz. Like the interpolated narratives, the documentary material serves a consistent thematic function but produces complications on the structural level.

VII

If we were to attempt at this point to construct a matrix of the novel as a whole, we would find that we need several graphs rather than just two axes. (See Appendix for actual diagrams.) If Franz's own story provides the main vertical axis, the chronology of the main action, then an analysis of the biblical allusions would produce a coherent progression with a parallel rhythm. We would find three main divisions that correspond structurally (i.e., they fall into the same pattern of paired books) to the three divisions of Franz's story as demonstrated by Ziolkowski. A graph of the literary allusions would also have three main divisions but these would be skewed slightly with Franz's development. The interpolated narratives and documentary material would show no coherent divisions at all. To regain the full view of Döblin's novel, we would have to lay each of our graphs etched on transparent sheets on top of one another. At first we would get a three-part division reinforced by different techniques, but eventually we would have so many dissonant patterns that our whole stack of graphs would reveal total greyness. The clarity of our basic rhythms would be obscured. Reified chaos indeed—but a chaos underpinned by a meaningful pattern of development.

Lest we lose sight of the pattern of development, Döblin provides a number of structural supports for it—the first of which is his narrator's introduction before Book I. With all the enthusiasm of a sports reporter at ringside, the narrator tells us how Franz is in a brutal boxing match with something that looks like fate. It knocks him down until at the end it seems that he is done for:

> Bevor er aber ein radikales Ende mit sich macht, wird ihm auf eine Weise, die ich hier nicht bezeichne, der Star gestochen. Es wird ihm aufs deutlichste klargemacht, woran alles lag. Und zwar an ihm selbst... (p. 7).

Before he makes a radical end of himself, however, his eyes are opened in a manner which I won't recount here. It is made extremely clear to him what everything depends on. Precisely on himself.

The narrator's enthusiasm overflows into his very language as he playfully rhymes "vollzogen/zurechtgebogen, lohnen/wohnen" (p. 7). The narrator goes on to describe Franz's violent cure and his eventual survival in the battering that life gives him, and concludes that Franz's story should be quite useful to those of us who live in a human skin and attempt, like Franz, to demand more from life than our bread and butter. The basic pattern, then, is loudly announced. Franz is expelled from the paradise of order and nonresponsibility represented by Tegel. He is tested three times, and finally destroyed to be reborn as a new and understanding man. The same pattern is reinforced through the poems introducing each book of the novel. Taken together these form a running summary very similar to that of the narrator's introduction but stressing more Franz's struggle to gain insight and his consequent rebirth.

Döblin, then, uses his narrator's introduction, the poems beginning each new book, biblical allusions and literary allusions to buttress the basic triadic rhythm of Franz's development. But over these he lays the complicating factors of interpolated narratives, documentary materials and narrator's digressions to produce a multilinearity of narrative voices and techniques, structural interferences, rhythmic contradictions that keep his novel on the level of modern relativity, that keep it from being simple "Bänkelgesang" or parable. The modern everyman must strive not just to fulfill stated rules but to understand that all rules are necessarily his own responsibility.

Only after Franz realizes that the problem was within himself, and accepts personal accountability for his life can he really be incorporated into the social community. The development is an extremely difficult one. *Berlin Alexanderplatz* is confusing and problematic like the modern world itself. Döblin discerns meaning in the world of modern Berlin, but he also recognizes the diversions, complications, digressions, and dissonances with which that world assaults its citizens and which cannot be resolved into a unilinear aesthetic unity. Döblin cannot, therefore, be a purely utopian writer; too much reality impinges upon his aesthetically structured solution. *Berlin Alexanderplatz* is caught in that tension, caught between the chaos of sensory perceptions of the external world and the inherent will to order, the aesthetic pattern of development which Döblin constructs. It is this struggle, this tension, which gives the book its real value—not the clever techniques as innovations in themselves, not the reification of chaos, but the impulse to resist it through aesthetic structure.

VIII

Finally, let us compare the overall structure of Döblin's *Berlin Alexanderplatz* to that of Dos Passos' *Manhattan Transfer*. First, Döblin uses a much more complex type of multilinearity, a more varied set of structural components in a sustained syncopation, than does Dos Passos. Rather than multiplying only the number of individual stories in his novel, Döblin increases the types of narrative voices, the various intrusions, allusions and interpolated commentary which convey the story of Franz Biberkopf. The multiplicity of narrative voices, often unidentifiable as discrete personalities or inseparable from the characters' own potential thoughts, creates a rather complex variation of the basic multilinear structure presented in Dos Passos' novel. Döblin expands the number of separate factors that must be considered in analyzing the structure of his novel. The center of thematic and structural gravity is, therefore, divided and dispersed over several books.

This more complex variety of the multilinear structure is part of the book's essential statement. The chaos of technique is meant to reify the frenetic chaos of modern urban life itself while opposing aesthetic order to that chaos. Franz Biberkopf must move with the speeding vehicles of the city, march with his fellows in a community of responsibility. Franz's mental level and social status may be low, but his environment is highly complex. Berlin does not allow for the patient repetition of situations and images over a twenty-five-year time span; it demands quickness, flexibility and, above all, resilience.

WILLIAM FAULKNER, 1933

IV
William Faulkner
As I Lay Dying

IN CONTRAST TO THE chaos of literary techniques and multiplicity of voices in *Berlin Alexanderplatz*, *As I Lay Dying* presents the rhetorically unadorned speeches of the farmers of Faulkner's fictional Yoknapatawpha county.[1] Even in comparison to Faulkner's own narrative works, *As I Lay Dying* displays little of the biblical and literary allusions that mark *Absalom, Absalom!* or *The Sound and the Fury*, its complexity occurring rather on the level of structure itself. In *As I Lay Dying*, Faulkner creates multilinearity by increasing the number of narrative points-of-view, by multiplying the actual number of discrete narrators. Some fifteen different speakers, appearing in unmediated juxtaposition, tell their own fragmentary versions of the burial journey of the Bundren family. They are not introduced or evaluated by any single controlling narrator. The reality that Faulkner conveys is the relativized, almost cubistic vision of a single activity from fifteen different narrative points-of-view.

I

Faulkner's 1930 tale of the death and burial of Addie Bundren is, on the surface, extremely fragmented and confusing. *As I Lay Dying* is composed of fifty-nine sections with fifteen different speakers but no single, objectively reliable narrator to provide the reader with dependable commentary. The novel is a prime example

of multiple narration without the guiding hand of an omniscient narrator. Whatever statement Faulkner wishes to make in the novel is made in the structural
arrangement itself.

When Addie Bundren extorts from her husband Anse the promise that he will
bury her with her kin in Jefferson, she sets in motion a series of events that will
involve the entire Bundren Family in a struggle for survival on the physical,
emotional, and interpersonal levels. Significantly, with her request Addie sets the
scene for her ultimate revenge for Anse's violation of her "aloneness" not on her
deathbed (as the novel's title would lead us to expect), but rather on the bed in
which she gives birth to Darl. In one way, it is Darl's entrance into the Bundren
Family which plants the seeds of its trials; it will be Darl's expulsion from the
family which ultimately permits it to survive. Darl and Addie, then, form the
nucleus of the plot. Addie's request precipitates the action of the central plot, the
fulfillment of the promise. Darl works continually to frustrate the completion of
the vow, to stop the irresistible motion that Addie begins.

This underlying network of tensions surfaces in the story of a rather primitive
farm family in Faulkner's mythical Yoknapatawpha County. The action begins as
Addie, the mother of the family, lies dying. Having ended her career as a country
school teacher to marry Anse, Addie suffers her whole life from her own too
perceptive consciousness and Anse's total insensitivity to both her and life in
general. Addie's passion for experiencing some redeeming moment of intense life
leads her to a relationship with Reverend Whitfield who is her son Jewel's real
father. This ultimate sin of the corruption of one sent to combat sin represents for
Addie a kind of salvation from the anesthetized existence of her husband Anse or
her Bible-thumping neighbor Cora.

Each of Addie's children reveals his personality by reacting to her death and
burial. Their lives are arranged around her. She is the focal point of the family
while she is alive, as she lies on her deathbed, and during her burial journey. Only
when Addie is buried and Darl is expelled from the family does Anse move to a
central position. While Addie awaits death, each of her children expresses his
relationship to her in an activity. Cash relentlessly and precisely shapes her coffin,
pausing only to display his work for her approval. Dewey Dell's fanning parallels
the consistent motion of Cash's saw as she hovers over Addie. Vardaman offers the
fruit of his activity, his fish, for Addie's inspection. Jewel in his savage attachment
to Addie would like to spirit her away to a protected hill where "It would be [him]
and her...and [Jewel] rolling the rocks down the hill at their faces, picking them up
and throwing them down the hill faces and teeth and all by God until she was quiet"
(p. 15).[2] Only Darl's actions run in a course away from Addie, as they will
throughout the novel. He takes Jewel to pick up a load of lumber thereby missing
Addie's moment of death although experiencing it perhaps more intensely in his

clairvoyant consciousness. Words, which Addie so mistrusts, do not come between Addie and her children. They are linked directly by actions, by "doing."

Sitting motionless on the front steps, only Anse resorts to words to predict doom, magnify his own suffering, and strike the martyr-like pose that induces everyone to help him against their will. Anse's words, punctuated occasionally by' his spitting into the dust, represent the very emptiness which Addie always resented in him. In her soliloquy she reflects:

> ...how words go straight up in a thin line, quick and harmless, and how terribly doing goes alone the earth, clinging to it, so that after a while the two lines are too far apart for the same person to straddle from one to the other; and that sin and love and fear are just sounds that people who never sinned nor loved nor feared have for what they never had and cannot have until they forget the words... (p. 165).

Anse himself identifies with the verticality of words in his analysis of God's creations, "when He aims for something to stay put, He makes it up-and-down ways, like a tree or a man" (p. 35). Anse in his vertical posture of undeserved abuse has never been able to straddle the gap between words and doing—either in his marriage to Addie or in his burial of her.

At Addie's death, the entire Bundren Family sets out for the Jefferson cemetery. Along the way each of her children will suffer harm or loss. Jewel will be deprived of his only interest in life besides Addie, his horse. Dewey Dell will lose ten dollars for her abortion pills and will, because of her näiveté, by robbed again of her already impaired virginity. Cash will lose the money for his phonograph and again suffer a broken leg. Vardaman will get to see neither the train in the store window nor his brother Darl in Jackson. And Darl must relinquish his sanity and his freedom. Only Anse emerges unscathed and triumphant from the journey—acquiring a phonograph, a new set of teeth, and a new wife as he is restored to the dominant position in the family.

Along the road from the Bundren farm to the cemetery at Jefferson, the family endures flood, fire, injury, compassion and callousness. Eventually, however, they do manage (with two spades borrowed from the future Mrs. Bundren) to get Addie buried. Within this surface story of individual human personality and its struggles, Faulkner evokes a deeper conflict of man with the irresistible forces and patterns of his history. This second level of meaning is built into the very structure of the novel.

II

Beginning the analysis of form on the most elementary level, we find the book divided into sections according to narrator. These sections do not present any immediately evident pattern. We note only that each section is headed by the name of the character who narrates it. That already implies some organization and at least one major component of Faulkner's overall concerns; he values the individual characters and their thoughts, their consciousness enough to give them structural prominence. In fact, the characters and their consciousness become one of the major structuring elements.[3] But what kind of structure do these fifteen disparate speakers provide?

To answer this question we must devise a method of keeping in view the fifteen disparate narrators in their relation to one another as well as the chronological development of the plot itself. To do this, it will be necessary to chart the fifty-nine sections of Faulkner's novel. We will borrow as our model the type of diagramming of a narrative tale employed by Claude Levi-Strauss in his study of the various versions of the Oedipus myth.[4] As I Lay Dying does actually present various versions of a particular story and, therefore, closely resembles the versions of a single myth which Levi-Strauss studies in his essay.[5]

To chart Faulkner's novel, I have systematically listed the order of appearance of the narrators (roughly equivalent to Levi-Strauss' enumerating the various versions of the Oedipus myth) on a horizontal axis and the order of sections, the plot as it unfolds, on the vertical axis. The chart is further divided on the vertical axis by major changes in setting and action in the course of the story. (See Diagram

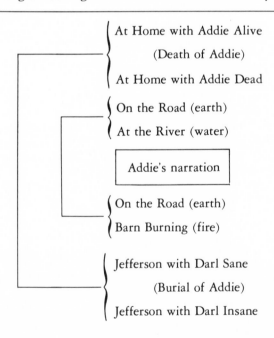

in the Appendix.) What we have done is to generate a graph, a visual summary of the sequence and juxtaposition or repetition or events and narrators and their interrelationship. This narrative matrix, which accounts for both the sequential (or temporal) and the spatial arrangement of the narrative, provides an analytic tool to aid in investigating what originally seemed a hopelessly complicated novel.

So far our critical analysis of structure has been purely descriptive. We must now make the critical leap from description to interpretation by plotting the narrative matrix to discover what Faulkner intended by placing Anse at the center of the horizontal (spatial) arrangement of his book while placing Addie's soliloquy at the center of the vertical (plot) pattern.

The matrix (which I have simplified by recording only the names of the narrators rather than all the incidents which my original chart included) reveals two separately motivated patterns. On the vertical axis, the matrix is divided by major changes in setting and action in the course of the story. These divisions reveal the symmetrical arrangement shown in the diagram on page 62. This pattern, motivated by plot and setting, is familiar as the typical progression in a mythic tale. The death of one of a society's prominent members (Addie) creates a lack or imbalance. An oath is made (to bury Addie). Trials must be undergone (here the mythic catastrophes of fire and flood). Eventually the oath is fulfilled (Addie is buried). The hero is rewarded (Anse gets a new wife and teeth—a symbol of renewed potency), and the social order (the integrity of the Bundren Family) is restored. The primary "hero" of this mythic plot is Anse, who successfully undertakes the fulfillment of the oath and is ultimately rewarded. The center of this symmetrical plot pattern, however, is not Anse but Addie, around whom all the action takes place.

Addie's central position is somewhat ironic. The pattern is motivated by plot, by occurring activity, and yet at its center is not a main *action*, but a still point of consciousness in Addie's soliloquy. Addie arises as the central consciousness, for her soliloquy alone of the Bundren's does not narrate the sequence of events.[6] Like Cora's immediately before it and Whitfield's after, Addie's speech is about the past, touching only on events before her death. Coming into the sequence of narrators eight days dead, she alone presents a completely disembodied, disinherited consciousness. Anyone still living has an interest in the Bundren's journey. Addie is the motivation for all her children to act; she organizes their present around her past. Although she is dead, she is not gone; she is yet the spirit of the Bundren children's present. She alone draws the reader away from the sequence of events and gives some explanation for them.

While she is alive, Addie does not figure as a consciousness available to the reader. She is seen entirely through her effect on the family. Her only words are Cash's name; otherwise, she dies in silence. Only after her death can she perform a narrative function, when the action of which she is the cause has already gone beyond the point of no return. Darl, whom Addie most resembles in her narrative style, becomes more and more certain that the terrible eternal task will be completed. His part in the novel after Addie's monologue is to become the inverse of Addie before the monologue. As Addie was the center of the family's collective consciousness before her death and the motivator of their action after it, Darl becomes their negative consciousness, their hinderer, attempting to delay or, better yet, completely halt the action. He knows that if the task is fulfilled, the archetypal pattern will make it impossible to "just ravel out into time" (p. 198). Darl fails in his attempt to perform a true act as a counterattack against the force of the pattern playing itself out. Jewel saves the corpse from the fire, as he saved it from the river.

When the Bundrens first reach Jefferson, Darl is still a part of the family, as Addie was in the first section of the book. But he is no longer an active sieve of consciousness. Like Addie giving up her will to live, Darl gives up his will to be aware and to fight against the forces in control of things. Like one of the non-kin narrators, in chapter fifty-two (p. 216) Darl adopts the tone of a neutral perceiver, seeing one act after another without comment.[7] For Addie's part to be played out fully, Darl—the successor to her all-encompassing and, therefore, threatening consciousness—must be expelled from the magic family circle. Addie's death is the paradox of time: in dying the death of time she initiates an eternal pattern of events. Darl's insanity is the inverse of her paradox: he continues to perceive the pattern working itself out against all obstacles, no longer resisting it, but unable to find a place in it.

III

It is inevitable with Faulkner that the line dividing event from consciousness is crossed. What began as an analysis of plot has become a description of a kind of symmetry of consciousness which some critics describe as the existential character of the novel.[8] This symmetry is not only thematic but actually a structural component of the novel. Returning to the matrix, we discover a second ordering principle. The mythic pattern motivated by plot (on the vertical axis) is countered by another symmetrical arrangement (on the horizontal axis) motivated by the order of appearance of the narrators from the Bundren family. This pattern is shown at the top of the horizontal axis and runs as follows:

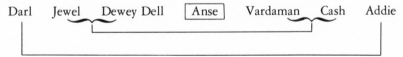

Darl   Jewel   Dewey Dell   │ Anse │   Vardaman   Cash   Addie

This arrangement discloses not a mythic plot pattern, but a range of potential of individual human consciousness.

The outside pair of Darl and Addie represents the most extensive individual consciousness. In fact, they represent the development of consciousness to the exclusion of physical well-being, since Addie dies and Darl goes insane. Darl and Addie are constantly expanding consciousness, moving from a knowledge of self in isolation to a perception of the super-individual patterns which make up all of existence. In her soliloquy Addie comes to realize that personal identity cannot be defined individually, by names, but rather identity is determined by shapes, by patterns bigger than the self. Her own pattern is to "get ready to stay dead a long time" (p. 167), to live out her life in order to die and be buried and thereby reinstitute the even larger mythic pattern. Darl, too, is first conscious of himself as an individual. He says, "Jewel and *I*" (p. 1), "I am *is*" (p. 76). His discrete individuality eventually gives way to a plurality of consciousness. Vardaman says, "But you *are*, Darl..." and Darl answers, "I know it...that's why I am not *is*" (p. 95). Darl would like his personal identity to be diffused in a larger pattern. "If you could just ravel out into time. That would be nice. It would be nice if you could just ravel out into time" (p. 198). Darl's final self-dissociation comes in his insanity.

Jewel, Dewey Dell, Vardaman, and Cash are aspects of a total consciousness of human life in action; their identities are functions of their consciousness. Jewel is entirely physical—he has only one brief narrative; he does not think in words. As Slabey concisely puts it, "Jewel is a 'doer'—he acts but does not think..."[9] His thoughts are incomplete until they are palpable, available to touch and wrestle with, first as his horse and then as the coffin. Dewey Dell is an historical consciousness; her life consists in the perception of her place in a pattern that recapitulates itself through time. She is not, like Addie, the cause of an eternal process, but simply another incarnation of it in time, a pawn aware of and finally reconciled to her bondage. Vardaman is the mythical consciousness. It is he who most easily accommodates himself to the pattern for not only does he not resist it, he infuses it with new life, creating a myth by himself—the myth of "My mother is a fish."[10] Vardaman successfully transfers his frustration and lack of understanding of his mother's death to a palpable object which is ritually consumed. Cash is a functional consciousness, speaking only when he has finished his work. When he has barely escaped drowning, the other characters risk their lives to save his tools, as if rescuing Cash's missing parts.

Finally, at the center of this symmetrical arrangement of possibilities of consciousness is Anse. He is so far from pure consciousness that one suspects complete lack of awareness behind the clichés of his speech. By placing Anse at the center of the pattern of consciousness, Faulkner creates a second ironic displacement that corresponds to that of Addie as the center of the mythic plot pattern. It is, after all, Addie's consciousness which is central and Anse's activity. This intentionally ironic displacement of centers provides both the major tensions and the major comedy of the novel. It points to the continual struggle of individual consciousness to accommodate itself to the irresistible mythic pattern in Addie while at the same time displaying in Anse the progress of an agonizingly un-extraordinary man to success and reward. In the midst of the struggles by others of more expanded consciousness to fix the present in a certain order so as to give it meaning, to resist the strangulation of indeterminate awareness, it is Anse's limited and direct consciousness which endures and triumphs.

IV

The structural analysis of the book has revealed two symmetrical arrangements: one which yields a mythic plot pattern and one which yields a range of individual consciousness. The main tension in the novel is precisely the struggle between the development of individual consciousness and the working out of the mythic pattern. This conflict reaches its climax in Dewey Dell's section, which is numerically the central narration (being number thirty of fifty-nine sections). This section represents the one moment of possible resolution in favor of the individual consciousness, the one point at which the mythic cycle could collapse and free the individuals caught in it. Dewey Dell could break the mythic pattern and end the mythic journey by asking Anse to turn off at New Hope Cemetery. But the mythic order itself encroaches upon her individual consciousness.

As Dewey Dell watches the sign for the New Hope turnoff, she undergoes an uncanny transformation, a kind of possession by Addie's ghost, which causes her to let the cemetery in New Hope, the one chance to break out of the established, old ordained pattern of events, slip by. Within three miles of the turnoff, the change begins:

> I heard that my mother is dead. I wish I had time to let her die. I wish I had time to wish I had. It is because in the wild outraged earth too soon, too soon, too soon. It's not that I wouldn't or will not it's that it is too soon, too soon, too soon. Now it begins to say it. New Hope three miles. New Hope three miles. *That's what they mean by the womb of time: the agony and the despair of the spreading bones, the hard girdle in which lie the outraged entrails of events...* (pp. 114-15).

The daughter becomes the mother almost immediately; she has no time to mourn or to find a personal identity for herself. From the moment of Addie's death Dewey Dell performs a function, keening over the corpse. The proper function, on the road past the New Hope turnoff, at the precise center of the book with twenty-nine narrations before and twenty-nine after, is to be Addie's avatar. As the possibility of being oneself with an insular identity comes ever closer as the New Hope, Addie's consciousness and vocabularly replace Dewey Dell's own: what was once just "a tub full of guts" (p. 56) is now "the hard girdle in which lie the outraged entrails of events," the concrete and limited personal mind spreading out into a larger, tragic consciousness. What Dewey Dell felt as an immediate fear ("I feel my body, my bones and flesh beginning to part and open upon the alone, the process of coming unalone is terrible" [p. 59]) here becomes a grudging vision of tragic order: "That's what they mean by the womb of time: the agony and despair of the spreading bones...."

The archetype of the mother, transferred from mother to daughter, teases Dewey Dell at the crossroads:

> *Suppose I tell him to turn. He will do what I say. Don't you know he will do what I say?* Once I waked with a black void rushing under me. I could not see. I saw Vardaman rise and go to the window and strike the knife into the fish, the blood gushing, hissing like steam but I could not see. *He'll do as I say. He always does. I can persuade him to anything. You know I can. Suppose I say turn here.* That was when I died that time. *Suppose I do. We'll go to New Hope! We don't have to go to town.* I rose and took the knife from the streaming fish still hissing and I killed Darl (p. 115).

It is Darl who makes Dewey Dell aware that she must lay down her life to an archetype, as it was Anse who made Addie realize it. At that time it was Addie who said, "Then I found that I had Darl. At first I would not believe it. Then I believed that I would kill Anse" (p. 164).

Darl's expulsion begins here. The daughter obeys and accepts the archetypal role not so much thrust upon her, or even placed on her shoulders, but found in what she once believed was her own body, transferred without anyone's knowledge or consent—except Darl's. Dewel Dell is at the center of the novel; the most important part of the pattern is completed here. Her center is Addie's as well; she is the prime mover of the journey. At first the most irresistible impulse to movement is Dewey Dell's wish to get to a drug store. But after section thirty she moves with her own force, as if she were already then certain that the child cannot be aborted. Finally, by informing on Darl to Gillespie, she causes Darl's removal and the success of the family's endurance. As the central narrator she is an aspect of Addie's central consciousness which presides over the stages of the plot.

What all this means, finally, is that the mythic pattern triumphs. The tensions between individual consciousness and the irresistible force of the mythic pattern that Faulkner has generated by the underlying structure of his novel is resolved ultimately in favor of myth. Society rights itself and maintains its continuity by completing the mythic progression. The dialectic tension created by the two axes of Faulkner's novel is resolved at the cost of the individual. For Faulkner the human state must be sustained within the mythic order and at the expense of the most highly developed individual consciousness. Therefore the consciousness of Darl and Addie, being too extensive, must be excluded from the family circle in order to maintain a viable social unit, in order for humanity to endure.

Faulkner has thus created a second order of meaning, a deeper plot, in the struggles generated by the structure of his novel. The problem of *As I Lay Dying* is not just the difficulties of getting Addie buried but also the difficulties of preserving the continuity of society in the face of the relativized visions of individual consciousness interacting with that of others. Faulkner's story is not just of the Bundrens or a poor Southern farm family but of the survival of human society itself—and the cost that that survival exacts from the most sensitive individuals. This story is told in the novel's very structure.

By examining the underlying ordering principles and relationships, implied by the originally simple matrix with which we opened this discussion of Faulkner's novel, we have arrived at an understanding of the essential concerns of the text. This investigation of the spatial arrangement of *As I Lay Dying* reveals that plot and consciousness, event and perception are inextricably entwined to create the total meaning of the novel. Initially vague intuitions that the reader has about a complicated text are thus made explicit and concrete.

V

Critics and readers of Faulkner will by this time be prepared to ask if my analysis implies a deliberate and *intentional* use of such a narrative matrix by Faulkner himself. Despite the valiant battle twentieth-century critics have waged against the "intentional fallacy," the question is unavoidable. It is also, at least from one point-of-view, irrelevant. Whether Faulkner actually had a carefully constructed narrative matrix (or something like it) in mind when he wrote *As I Lay Dying* is, of course, impossible to determine with any assurance. That he was aware of the basic components of that matrix in his novel is evident from his remarks in 1956 when he stated:

> I simply imagined a group of people and subjected them to the simple universal natural catastrophes, which are flood and fire, with a simple natural motive to give direction to their progress.[11]

Whether Faulkner consciously manipulated the patterns I have proposed in the book, however, I cannot answer. That the patterns are there and do generate meaning cannot easily be refuted.

We can, further, determine that the structural components of an irresistible, recurrent mythic pattern of events and of a range of human consciousness reacting to those events are common to several of Faulkner's works. *Absalom, Absalom!* and *The Sound and the Fury* are both based on the theme of a larger recurrent pattern struggling to subsume the identity of the individual. Many critics have noted these components by pointing out Faulkner's use of pattern and archetype as well as his interest in structure itself.[12] There is, then, already a critical consensus that all essential components of the structural analysis are readily discernible in Faulkner's works: the struggle of individual consciousness to establish a discrete identity, the constant recurrence of large patterns of meaning (historical or mythic), and the basic preoccupation with the creation of meaning through structure itself. What I hope to have added to Faulkner scholarship in my analysis is a more concrete basis for the subjective feelings that the reader and critic have as to how those components fit together, as to precisely how Faulkner generates the tensions and humor of his novels through form.

More specifically, this study corroborates on a concrete level several interpretations developed from more thematic points-of-view. Slabey's analysis of the attitudes of the various Bundrens toward the problems of existence, for example, parallels quite closely the pairings suggested by the horizontal axis of the narrative matrix. Slabey allies Addie and Darl, Dewey Dell and Vardaman as facing "'the ontological mystery'—metaphysical problems of being and non-being, existence and essence."[13] He pairs Cash and Jewel as operating on a primarily physical level and singles out Anse as depending entirely on the verbal approach.[14] This grouping, which Slabey derives from his reading of the novel as an existentialist work, is verified by the structural arrangement presented here. Slabey further notes the ties between Addie and Dewey Dell[15] which we have examined. Secondly, the structural analysis links the preoccupation of Bradford, Monaghan, and Lilly with Addie's centrality to the actual physical arrangement of the vertical axis of the matrix while demonstrating in the structural irony of the two axes the necessary limits or complements to Addie's central position. Finally, the discovery of a mythic pattern built into the very structure of the work helps explain the critical tendency to seek correspondences between the Bundrens and classical or biblical figures on the part of Gold, Collins, Kerr, and Sanderlin, although it does not particularly support any specific correspondence.

This structural study, then, provides a useful key not only to the work itself but also to the various critical impulses it has triggered. It defines more concretely the basis of the thematic and philosophical concerns of the work and the underlying factors of its critical reception.

VI

The final question is how to categorize the type of structure which Faulkner has used to create meaning in *As I Lay Dying*. First, for all the complexity and profundity which it generates, the overall structure of the novel is relatively simple. It consists, basically, of two major components which can be presented as a two-dimensional matrix. The complexity of those two components, however, lends the book its richness and depth. They are highly abstract and are freighted with all the cultural and psychological connotations of profound abstractions as well as reinforced by rhetorical richness. Faulkner uses an ever-recurrent mythic pattern in opposition to the attempt of a multiplicity of individual consciousness to create and maintain a discrete, personal identity. He could not have chosen a "simple conflict" more central to the cultural history of Western civilization. The Greeks, Nietzsche and Freud would all readily acknowledge the importance of Faulkner's structural components. Despite the seeming confusion of fifty-nine chaotic sections of narration, *As I Lay Dying* presents a rather "elegant" (in the scientific or mathematical sense of the simplest formulation that accounts for the widest range of variables) arrangement of two highly abstract and profound components.

In comparison to the two earlier works we have analyzed, Faulkner's novel represents a further variation on the idea of multilinearity. *As I Lay .Dying* presents an economical two-dimensional structure within which the number of discrete narrators is greatly increased. The structural components of Döblin's and Dos Passos' novels were greater in number than Faulkner's two basic principles. They were more concrete—allusions, documentary material, newspaper ads, songs—but at the same time less profound than the structural components of *As I Lay Dying*. Overall the structures of *Berlin Alexanderplatz* and *Manhattan Transfer* are both looser and more complicated than that of Faulkner's novel. Their centers of thematic and structural gravity are dispersed whereas here they are concentrated in the centripetal force of Addie's burial. Dos Passos uses the mosaic pieces of the life stories of many characters to create a picture of Manhattan. Döblin's work is built of the composite action of many discrete literary techniques. Faulkner, in contrast, creates a complexity of two basic components. The multiplicity of his various narrators is welded into a single overriding tension of individual human consciousness seeking to escape a repetition that surpasses the simple reiteration of situations and images in *Manhattan Transfer* to reach an ineluctable mythic recurrence. Faulkner's multilinearity, finally, taps a deeper source of tradition and cultural meaning than either Dos Passos' or Döblin's.

WOLFGANG KOEPPEN, 1960's

V
Wolfgang Koeppen
Tauben im Gras

IN THE PRECEDING three chapters we have examined works of a relatively brief historical period. *Manhattan Transfer, Berlin Alexanderplatz*, and *As I Lay Dying* were all published in the five years from 1925 to 1930. What we discovered was a diversity of experiments all employing multilinear structures of varying complexity. Writing at approximately the same time, Dos Passos, Döblin and Faulkner propose three different responses to the demise of the omniscient narrator and the tradition he represented. Faulkner chooses to build the thematic tension of his novel into a two-dimensional narrative matrix of simple structure but with a high degree of abstract profundity. Döblin selects a much more complicated arrangement, playing each of his narrative techniques against the main plot line of the Biberkopf story, and produces a multidimensional matrix of paired, concrete components (e.g., biblical allusions vs. Franz's personal development). In *Berlin Alexanderplatz* Döblin pits an underlying aesthetic order against the chaos of big city reality. Dos Passos also deals with big city chaos in *Manhattan Transfer*; his presentation, however, is essentially different in structure and aim from Döblin's. Like Döblin, Dos Passos sees a kind of order amid the chaos of urban life, but it is an existential rather than an aesthetic order. A precisely repeated pattern of situations and images emerges in Dos Passos' novel, but it represents the inescapable and meaningless waste of human potential. Across all the disconnected lives of the many characters of Dos Passos' book runs an underlying pattern not of hope but of despair

A synchronic view, then, discloses a great deal of diversity in novels which share the use of multilinear structures. But what happens to the multilinear novel later in the century? Do these structural innovations mellow into a tradition of novel writing or do they merely fade into their own creative fancy, a momentary fad in literary history? It would be interesting to follow the development of this type of structurally complex, fragmentary, multilinear narrative work step-by-step. Such a study would yield a good deal of information about the evolution of literary forms and the course of literary history and it would help to answer various questions. One could examine whether the multilinear novels appear in times of particular cultural or historical stress; whether they have a limited number of possible variations; and whether they possess a cross-cultural appeal. One could ask if the French *nouveau roman* writers could be fitted into the overall picture of development. These issues will provide fields of research for the future. But for the present, let us continue in our more limited view of the situation by examining one more recent novel definitely within the multilinear tradition. After having progressed five years from *Manhattan Transfer* in 1925 to *As I Lay Dying* in 1930, let us leap forward some twenty-five years to Wolfgang Koeppen's *Tauben im Gras* of 1951.[1]

Koeppen's novel is particularly relevant to our study for several reasons. First, it shares a number of features with the books already examined.[2] Like *Berlin Alexanderplatz* and *Manhattan Transfer*, Koeppen's novel focuses on characters within a big city. Like the third section of *Manhattan Transfer*, it examines a postwar era. The montage of real and fictitious news headlines, of popular songs, of historical background facts as well as the juxtaposition of many discrete sections of narration are all techniques which clearly mark *Tauben im Gras* as one of the hiers to the earlier multilinear tradition. Second, Koeppen clearly sees himself as belonging to the tradition of structural innovation begun by Joyce, Dos Passos, Döblin and others. In an interview with Horst Bienek in 1961 Koeppen commented: "Ich bin überzeugt, daß man heute auch ohne die Wegmarke Joyce in seine Richtung gehen müßte.... Dieser Stil entspricht unserem Empfinden, unserem Bewußtsein, unserer bitterer Erfahrung."[3] ("I am convinced that even without the guidepost of Joyce, one today would have to go in his direction.... This style corresponds to our consciousness, our bitter experience.")

Surprisingly enough, Koeppen's novel bears a particularly close thematic and structural resemblance to the work most removed from it temporally, Dos Passos' *Manhattan Transfer*. Appearing a quarter of a century and one World War apart, the two novels share a remarkable number of characteristic themes. Both novels are built on the concept of a cross-section of urban life. Becker pointed this out in *Manhattan Transfer* and Manfred Koch makes much the same observation about *Tauben im Gras:*

Diese Fülle von über dreißig Personen und mehr als zwanzig Schauplätzen ist in keine einsinnig durcherzählte Geschichte gezwängt worden, und ein dominierendes äußeres Geschehen mit einigen wenigen Hauptfiguren läßt sich nicht mehr herauslösen. Andere Intentionen als im konventionellen Roman werden hier offensichtlich aufzudecken sein. Der Autor selbst sagte zu Bienek, daß er "ein Pandämonium im Sinn" (60) gehabt habe, das heißt, die "Versammlung aller guten und bösen Geister" soll im Roman arrangiert werden.

Sicherlich wird schon durch die Anzahl der Figuren dem Leser signalisiert, daß der Roman um keinen "Helden" kreist, dessen Lebensgeschichte den "Inhalt" ausmacht. Stattdessen treten viele Personen auf, die durch Altersunterschiede (man denke an die Kinder Hilegonda, Heinz und Ezra, die Jugendlichen Schorschi, Bene, Kare und Sepp einerseits, an die Kinderfrau Emmi oder den Dienstmann Josef andererseits), durch Schichtenzugehörigkeit (den mittellosen Jugendlichen stehen etwa der Filmstar Alexander und der reiche Dichter Edwin gegenüber), Nationalität (neben den Deutschen finden wir vor allem Amerikaner in der besetzten Stadt) und durch Rasse (Odysseus Cotton ist Neger, Henriette Galligher Jüdin, die meisten anderen sind Weisse) einen Bevölkerungsquerschnitt Nachkriegsmünchens repräsentieren. Mit keinem "Einzel- oder Familienschicksal" könnte eine ähnliche Vielfalt der städtischen Gesellschaft eingefangen werden.[4]

This abundance of over thirty characters and more than twenty settings is not forced into any unambiguous story told all the way through, and a dominant, external series of events with a few main figures is no longer discernable. Obviously other intentions than those of the conventional novel are to be uncovered here. The author himself said to Bienek, that he had had "a pandamonium in mind," that is, the "assembly of all good and evil spirits" is supposed to be arranged in the novel.

Surely, the very multitude of characters signals the reader that the novel does not center on any "hero" whose life's story forms the "content" of the book. Instead, many people come forward who represent a cross section of the population of post war Munich according to differences in age (consider the children Hilegonda, Heinz and Ezra, the teenagers Schorschi, Bene, Kare and Sepp on the one hand, and the governess Emmi or the servant Josef on the other), in class (the destitute teenagers contrast with the filmstar Alexander and the rich poet Edwin), in nationality (after the Germans we find predominantly Americans in the occupied city), and in race (Odysseus Cotton is Black, Henriette Galligher a Jewess, most of the others are white). No single story of an individual's or family's fate could encompass a similar multiplicity of urban society.

The two novels share the basic multilinear structure that juxtaposes a number of different characters and their life stories. Both authors are interested in the isolated desperation and self-involvement of the many characters, in what Stanley Craven refers to as their "lack of contact,"[5] although they display an essential difference in the nature of that isolation. Both novels examine the effects of past memories, of environment, and inherited social position on the present capacity of the characters to cope with realities of their situations. In *Manhattan Transfer* Dos Passos frequently traces a character's development from its childhood beginnings, covering a period of nearly twenty-five years in the narrated material. Koeppen, on the other hand, limits his narrated time span to less than twenty-four hours (approximately eighteen hours from just before early mass to midnight of the same day, a time period which parallels Joyce's eighteen hours in the Dublin of *Ulysses*). The memories of Koeppen's characters, however, greatly expand the actual narrated time.

Sharing all these characteristics and concerns with the earlier works, Koeppen's *Tauben im Gras* will provide a later example of the multilinear tradition we have been studying and will enable us to propose a few tentative hypotheses of a generic and historical nature.

I

Ending Koeppen's twenty-year silence, *Tauben im Gras* deals with the lives of some thirty characters in the large German city of Munich not long after World War II, during the economic, spiritual, and emotional recovery from the devastation of the war. Many of the city's buildings still lie in ruins; poverty and inflation are still daily problems; American occupation troops are painfully omnipresent. The people still live under the threat of renewed conflicts. But they live also with the desire to forget, to regain some kind of security and happiness in life on a personal and national level. As Koch points out, the characters range in social class from baggage carriers and prostitutes to the old wealthy families ruined by the war to the nouveaux riches of entertainers and industrialists. The characters also span a cultural range from American Negro Southerners to white Californians, German nationalists, Czech expatriots, and a range of German-American combinations.

To attempt to summarize a plot of the thirty different stories that make up the novel would be somewhat like trying to summarize an encyclopedia. There are, however, a few main plot lines to which the secondary characters are tied more or less loosely. The story of the frustrated German author Philipp and his wife Emilia, who is hopelessly ensnared in memories of her wealthy childhood, is linked to the visiting lecturer Mr. Edwin, an American author of world renown who has come to resurrect the "Geist" of Germany by retracing her cultural heritage. Philipp and Emilia live in a continual psychological and emotional battle with each other and within themselves. Neither can really adjust to a role in a defeated Germany which is economically and spiritually bankrupt. Mr. Edwin, who fails to adjust his cultural ideals to the reality of a devastated city, is mugged by a teenage gang while envisioning himself as a combination of Alcibides and Socrates.

A second main plot concerns the black American soldier Washington Price and the German woman, Carla, who bears his child. An idealist baseball star, Washington dreams of opening an inn in which "no one is undesirable," in which the racial and religious discrimination he has experienced his entire life will be counteracted by a racially and culturally mixed family. Running somewhat parallel to Washington's story is that of Odysseus Cotton, another black American soldier who makes love to a German woman and kills an old German porter, Josef.

Tied to these main stories are several connected storylines such as that of Carla's divorced mother and father and that of Carla's son Heinz and his interaction with the American-born Ezra, whose mother's family was killed by the Nazis. Richard Kirsch, an American-German, is also related to Carla's family by birth. In addition, the theatrical family of Messalina and Alexander, their daughter Hellegonda and her nurse Emmi, tie several of the characters together as Messalina searches the city for people to invite to her party that evening. Dr. Behude also links several characters as he treats them as patients in his psychiatric practice.

What these many secondary relationships reveal is an aspect of *Tauben im Gras* that makes it distinctly different from *Manhattan Transfer* and links it more clearly, perhaps, to some of Virginia Woolf's work. The seemingly discrete lives of various characters in Koeppen's novel begin to overlap and cling to one another as the book progresses. Whereas Dos Passos frequently introduces characters in *Manhattan Transfer* who never meet one another or who, in fact, never appear again in the book, Koeppen carefully, if sometimes tenuously, links his characters to each other—either by family relationships, physical encounters, or interest in the same objects. This last technique of interpersonal linking occurs among several of the main characters; e.g., Mr. Edwin inspects a madonna that once belonged to Philipp and sees Emilia trying to sell another of Philipp's treasures, a cup with a portrait of a German king—eventually purchased by Ezra's father Christopher for his wife Henrietta. In a similar situation, Emilia gives a piece of jewelry to the young American school teacher, Kay. She, in turn, eventually leaves the jewelry with Philipp, whom she believes to be a starving artist, while they both listen to Mr. Edwin's cries for help as he is mugged. Or again, Emilia takes in the dog which Carla's son, Heinz had intended to sell to Christopher's son, Ezra.

All of these complicated relationships reveal a tenuous unity of urban characters in *Tauben im Gras* that was not evident in the isolated lives of many of Dos Passos' characters in *Manhattan Transfer*. The question remains, however, whether that unity provides a kind of security and consolation or merely a more intricate form of inescapable entrapment.

II

Tauben im Gras consists of 103 individual sections of narrative.[6] These are not separated into distinct chapters or sections as in Döblin's or Dos Passos' works, but flow continuously in an uninterrupted juxtaposition of discrete passages reminiscent of the organization of Faulkner's *As I Lay Dying*. This uninterrupted flow, like blood relationships and objects viewed in common, helps to unite the seemingly isolated characters by involving them in a common narrative space.

The order of those individual passages begins to imply further structuring principles. The two opening passages of the novel, which do not involve any of the main human characters, introduce the city itself. The first image portrays a city caught in the memory of past conflict and destruction but attempting to get on with the business of living. The drone of airplanes over the city reminds people of the war, but they no longer need to look up in fear. The second passage emphasizes the modern urban man's dependence on technology, on power and fuel, by focusing on the machines necessary to keep an urban center functioning and on the newspaper sellers who keep the city informed. The image of the newspaper dealers and the planes will be picked up again in the very last passage of the novel as the occurrences of the day are concretized into the print of the daily newspapers just as the lives of Koeppen's characters are solidified into the print of his novel.

By bracketting his novel with passages which repeat images of dehumanized technology and degraded language, Koeppen establishes, by structural implication, the constant problems of the urban center. He also points to the continuing difficult position of urban dwellers who face the additional hardship of living in a city devastated by the war. The same technology and propaganda which helped to fuel the war machine must now be accepted by the population in order to re-establish the city as a living entity. By placing these strategic passages at the opening and closing of his novel, Koeppen keeps the framework of the effect of war on urban dwellers constantly in the reader's consciousness.

Another note sounded in the two opening passages is repeated at the book's close. The omnipresent tension of the postwar period is evoked to stress the tentative, insecure life of the city as well as the torn and ruptured state of Germany itself:

> *Spannung, Konflikt,* man lebte im Spannungsfeld, östliche Welt, westliche Welt, man lebte an der Nahtstelle, vielleicht an der Bruchstelle, die Zeit war kostbar, sie war eine Atempause auf dem Schlachtfeld, und man hatte noch nicht richtig Atem geholt...sie ließen weiter zerbrechen, was schon angebrochen war: Deutschland war in zwei Teile gebrochen.... Die Flieger, die am Himmel rumorten, waren die Flieger der andern (pp. 11-12).

Tension, Conflict, people lived in a high tension grid, eastern world, western world, they lived at the seam, perhaps at the point of rupture, time was precious, it was a momentary respite on the battle field, and one hadn't yet really caught his breath.... What was already breaking was permitted to be fractured: Germany was broken into two pieces.... The flyers who roared in the skies were the flyers of the others.

The same image is repeated and intensified as the novel closes, again pointing to the ongoing tension and rupture in Germany after the war. As in *Manhatten Transfer,* so exact a repetition of images at the opening and close of the novel implies an inescapable sameness that encompasses all the seemingly idiosyncratic dramas of individual lives. And as in Dos Passos' work, the repetition is not a consolation but an imprisonment. Men are caught in a setting they can neither escape nor change—like Philipp, who as a German author refuses to pander to popular tastes but does not have the power to change them. The city, the nation of Germany is caught in an historic circumstance it can neither control nor alter.[7] The only choice open to Germany and her people is to endure as gracefully and happily as possible.

Another reference that Koeppen's city novel shares with Dos Passos' is the comparison to Babylon and Nineveh—with the addition in the more recent novel of Sodom. In the ninth and eleventh narrative passages, those who fled the cities return as the war years recede, but they return to a site of burning asphalt and "stygian water." The city is now depicted as a place to die, embittered and anonymous, and engulfed in gasoline vapors and the noise of streetcars. The city creatures return to their concrete and asphalt environments, their own Babylon, Nineveh and Sodom. One is tempted to ask, then, if the city represents some demonic force for Koeppen as it had for many of the earlier expressionist poets,[8] if it is the city itself which corrupts. For Dos Passos the city was largely indifferent, enduring beyond the individual lives it contained but not really contributing to their demise. In *Manhattan Transfer* man does himself in. I would suggest that the same holds true for *Tauben im Gras.* Man creates his own hell, which becomes concentrated by the physical proximity provided by the city. The two passages discussed above flank a section concerning Dr. Behude's patients, who are masters at creating and sustaining their own psychological Babylons. This section becomes a kind of litany of impaired human beings, of neurotics, liars, homosexuals, pedophiliacs, as well as of artists, writers, and actors whose craft has been choked to death by modern life. The list emphasizes the fact that it is not some expressionist monster of technology and power which devours men; they are quite capable of devouring themselves psychologically. As in Dos Passos' work, it is not the city alone which is the problem, but the torments of life which are portrayed in a more concentrated form in the urban setting.

III

One particularly prominent technique of self-destruction in Koeppen's book is that of building one's life and hopes on a dead illusion of the past. Emilia, perhaps more than any other character, specializes in this practice. Heiress to a large fortune in pre-war Germany, she emerges from the war with all the habits of wealth but without the means of supporting them. She is tied to now worthless jewels and real estate which no one wants to buy. She feels personally affronted by the war, by her husband, who fails to become a rich and successful author and thus give her the security and wealth she craves, and by life in general, which obstinately refuses to conform to her memories of a glorious past. Emilia spends all her time trying to relive her memories and to forget the war that destroyed them. She indulges in total self-involvement, symbolized at one point by her masturbating in an attempt to gain emotional release from the realities of her degraded life. The total self-involvement of the masturbation, however, does not release Emilia from the remembrance of her lost past for more than the few moments it takes to carry out.

But Emilia is not alone in her illusions and distress. Other characters operate in much the same way. Alexander and Messalina live in the constant illusion of the movie world. Frau Behrend endures in the illusion that the world somehow owes her a continued existence. Wiggerl, Shorshi, Bene, Kare and Sepp labor under the myth that "a soldier's death is the most beautiful death" while they sit in the darkness of the movie theater viewing "Der letzte Bandit." The Massachusetts school teacher Kay tours war-torn Germany envisioning encounters with poets in romantic German forests. Perhaps the most disturbing illusions, however, are those entertained by Philipp and Mr. Edwin.

As writers, Philipp and Mr. Edwin are, in a sense, the keepers of the common goods, the preservers of culture. Their illusions, therefore, imply a much broader hypocrisy, a broader failure of the ideal, of the dream, to affect reality. Both Philipp and Mr. Edwin still consider the writer to be a powerful cultural figure. On a personal level, however, each of them fails. Philipp, who refuses to sink to the level of writing popular trash for Alexander and his film crew, is just as unable as Mr. Edwin to reform the popular tastes, to upgrade the post-war cultural level of the common man. In a moment of devastating candor Philipp expresses his personal failure, "...unfähig, feige, überflüssig bin ich: ein deutscher Schriftsteller" (p. 60). ("...incapable, cowardly, superfluous is what I am: a German author.") But the personal failure is generalized here—"ein deutscher Schriftsteller." Philipp's own disillusionment and incapacities are extended to German letters on a larger scale.

Edwin faces much the same realization in his moments of candid self-doubt. He has come to resurrect the trampled German spirit but he wonders if he really has anything to offer, anything at all to say to these people. The reader can only wonder, too, as the majority of Edwin's audience sleeps, daydreams or chats through his lecture. Mr. Edwin himself feels the impotence of his words, drowned and deformed in the drone of a faulty loud-speaker system. Edwin's grand illusion is one of meaning in general: his effort is to counter Gertrude Stein's and Hemingway's realizations of meaninglessness as he quotes the novel's title:

> Wie Tauben im Gras, sagte Edwin, die Stein zitierend, ...wie Tauben im Gras betrachteten gewisse Zivilisationsgeister die Menschen, indem sie sich bemühten, das Sinnlose und scheinbar Zufällige der menschlichen Existenz bloßzustellen, den Menschen frei von Gott zu schildern, um ihn dann frei im Nichts flattern zu lassen, sinnlos, wertlos, frei und von Schlingen bedroht, dem Metzger preisgegeben, aber stolz auf die eingebildete, zu nichts als Elend führende Freiheit von Gott und göttlicher Herkunft. Und dabei, sagte Edwin, kenne doch schon jede Taube ihren Schlag und sei jeder Vogel in Gottes Hand (p. 221).

> Like pigeons in the grass, said Edwin, quoting Stein, ...certain spirits of civilization regarded men as pigeons in the grass in that they attempted to lay bare the senseless and ostensibly accidental nature of human existence, to depict men free of God, only to let him flutter free in the abyss, senseless, without value, free and threatened by snares, given up to the butcher, but proud of the imagined freedom from God and divine origin, which led to nothing but misery. And nevertheless, said Edwin, each pigeon knows its loft and each bird rests in God's hand.

These sentiments of Stein were expressed earlier by the singularly illusion-free Miss Burnett as she watched sparrows on the lawn. Stein, Hemingway and Miss Burnett win out, however, as Edwin's life comes to an end at the hands of a band of boys amid Germany's ruins. Picturing himself as a combination of Socrates and Alcibides, Edwin encounters the immoveable reality of a street gang. While he muses over the Platonic soul in the boys who prepare to attack him, they see only an old fool ready to be robbed and beaten. The disparity in the two visions emphasizes Edwin's ultimate impotence in the real world, his inability to comprehend on what level the crowds of mankind are generally operating. In one final unbearable moment of illusion reminiscent of the death of Thomas Mann's Aschenbach, Edwin thinks of how "proud and beautiful" the gang of boys is which is in the process of taking his life. Edwin perishes amid his illusions, and the hopeful sentiments he presented for the larger world perish with him.

The reader begins to wonder in this morass of personal delusions if perhaps "der Schläfer," the drug addict Schnakenback, is not right in thinking man only some unsolved, momentous chemical equation. Koeppen does present, however, one overriding counterdream, a benevolent illusion of future reconciliation in the story of Carla and Washington Price. Washington, raised in the South where signs of "Blacks Not Allowed" or "Whites Unwanted" dominated his childhood, went to war against those who ostracized the Jews. Although Koeppen too easily equates racial prejudices of America with the death camps and systematized persecution of the Jews in World War II, his juxtaposition of bigotries is a rather devastating indictment of the crusader-savior Americans. But the black American who chooses a white German wife possesses the ultimate dream of human unity and dignity. His and Carla's unborn child is Washington's concrete proof of the possibility of his dream. And Koeppen respects and protects this one benevolent illusion from Carla's personal fears and abortion attempts and from the stones of a drunken, misled mob.

IV

Washington and Carla are among the very few characters who succeed in establishing a real relationship. In a novel riddled with the divorce of the Behrends, Carla's dead spouse, the failed encounter of the idealistic young American Kay and the disillusioned German poet Philipp, the relationship of the lesbian Messalina and her impotent husband Alexander, and the marriage of Philipp and Emilia, who are among the few characters in the book who are never physically brought together—those couples who do manage to relate to one another on some meaningful level stand out even more prominently. There are really only three such couples: Carla and Washington, Herr Behrend and Vlasta, and Odysseus Cotton and the prostitute, Susanne. Each of these couples represents a union of apparently irreconcilable characteristics.

Perhaps the strangest of the three is the violent, emotional, sexual relationship of the black American soldier Odysseus Cotton and the German prostitute Susanne. Not only does this couple share with Washington and Carla the racial merging of black and white and the national merging of American and German, this unlikely couple also unifies the cultural traditions of classical Greece and the Old Testament. When the reader first meets Susanne in Alexander's bathroom after her unexpected lesbian experience with Messalina and Alfreda, Koeppen quips, "Susanne im Bade," the Old Testament Susanne in the bath. Later in the novel when Susanne encounters Odysseus Cotton, the narrator comments, "Susanne, who was Circe and the Sirens and perhaps even Nausikaa." Susanne plays a Greek role to Odysseus Cotton, who himself enbodies both the Greek cultural heritage and the American economic environment suggested by his name. This already entangled relationship is further complicated by the fact that Susanne robs Odysseus when they first meet, thus precipitating Odysseus' murder of the baggage carrier Josef. This act, however, only ties her more closely to Odysseus in a bond of common alienation. Susanne is drawn to Odysseus because she recognizes in him a fellow pariah, who in his lawlessness and murder strikes a blow against the society which rejects them both. Born of desperation and violence, Odysseus' and Susanne's relationship is, nevertheless, one of the few successful unions in the book. Ostracism and despair and violence apparently represent one way to reconcile disparate traditions. But, appropriately, the union is consummated in the tottering ruins that remain of Germany's attempt to force world unity through violence, ostracism, and brutality. Black and white flesh finally unite amidst the bombed-out buildings of the city which would never again arise as it had stood before the war. These two, entwined on the brink of the abyss left by the devastation of battle, may be the real incarnation of Edwin's vision of cultural unity.

Herr Behrend and his love Vlasta present a more hopeful union. The Obermusikmeister Behrend appears conducting a jazz ensemble in the black American soldiers' club. During the war he met and fell in love with a Czech girl, Vlasta, who hid him from the enemy and fled with him back to Germany despite all social pressures. In one sense, Herr Behrend and Vlasta parallel Odysseus and Susanne by being socially ostracized. They relinquish national, family, and social ties to be together, but they are the only couple in the entire novel clearly depicted as happy and secure in each other's love:

> Vlasta hatte sich von allem losgesagt; sie hatte sich von ihrem Vaterland losgesagt; und Herr Behrend hatte sich von vielem losgesagt; er hatte sich von seinem ganzen bisherigen Leben losgesagt: sie fühlten sich beide losgelöst, sie waren frei, sie waren glücklich. Sie hätten es vorher nicht für möglich gehalten, daß man so frei und so glücklich sein könne (p. 200).

> Vlasta had renounced everything; she had renounced her homeland, and Herr Behrend had renounced much; he had renounced his entire life to this point: they both felt released, they were free, they were happy. They never would have thought it possible beforehand that one could be so free and so happy.

These two accomplish what Emilia and Philipp and Edwin will never accomplish —they cut their lives loose from the past and from all social mores. They find happiness and security amid a tenuous existence by doing so.

The final successful couple, Washington Price and Carla Behrend, also succeed in sundering past fetters and surrendering national and social ties in order to be together. They plan to go to Paris to establish "Washington's Inn," the haven of an existence which is to be prejudice-free. Thus they will both leave their native country in order to find a place where only individual human worth is valued. Theirs is not an easy union. Carla nearly succeeds in attaining the abortion that would have shattered Washington's dream forever. But they struggle back to the possibility of the ideal; Carla believes in Washington and his dream. She shows herself to be her father's daughter, as her mother had earlier lamented. She and Washington succeed in uniting white and black, German and American in a relationship of love and hope. They will experience hardship and strife, but their lives are not tied in the despair and violence of Odysseus' and Susanne's existence. They represent a union of hope that counterbalances the union of Odysseus and Susanne.

The one thing that all three couples share, however, is their outcast, ostracized status. Odysseus and Susanne stand outside of both German and American society by virtue of their crimes. Herr Behrend and Vlasta voluntarily leave their societies. And Washington and Carla will be exiled from both German and American culture. For Koeppen's post-war world, the cost of personal happiness seems necessarily to entail social and cultural alienation. A return to individual, personal values which cut out nationalistic thinking, cultural snobbism and racial bigotry represents the only successful way of life. The strong individual cut loose from the fetters of his environment can survive. Koeppen's characters have at least that hope—they have a tentative survival policy that puts them in a somewhat more comfortable position than Dos Passos' characters in *Manhattan Transfer*. The repetition of national and racial mixture in these three couples becomes a reiteration of hope amid the moldering world of Emilia and Philipp's despair.

This interpersonal salvation proposed by Koeppen in *Tauben im Gras* represents, however, an existential rather than a political solution. For all of the political references and backgrounding in the novel, one is forced, finally, to agree with Klaus Haberkamm's evaluation that the work is:

> ...Erzählung von Schicksal, Angst, Zweifel, Vergangenheit und Aussichtslosigkeit, kein politischer, sondern ein existentialistisch-anthropologisch ausgerichteter und damit mythischer Roman.[9]

> ...a story of fate, fear, doubt, the past and hopelessness, not a politically, but an existentially-anthropologically designed, and therefore mythical novel.

Much like Dos Passos and Döblin before him, Koeppen offers not a specifically political but rather an individual solution to modern cultural chaos.

The very structural arrangement of the book discloses the counterbalancing of the two basic thematic impulses of predominating social negativity and individual hope. Emilia's and Philipp's stories occupy a number of central passages. Interspersed among these darker sections are the hopeful struggles of Washington and Carla, Herr Behrend and Vlasta. The diagram in the Appendix reveals how tightly these two opposite patterns are interlocked. They run in a constant criss-crossing, a complex balance that tips finally to the more pessimistic vision of meaninglessness, but that is never wholly given over to despair.

V

In addition to these heterosexual couples, the novel also presents several unisexual pairs. I am not thinking of the homosexual relationships in which the book abounds, such as Jack and Hänschen, Messalina and Alfreda, and possibly on a repressed level Miss Wescott and Kay. I am thinking rather of the pairs of *Doppelgänger* in the novel: Philipp and Mr. Edwin; Emilia and Kay, Messalina and her own second self; Heinz and Ezra.

The most striking and obvious of the *Doppelgänger* pairs is that of Mr. Edwin and Philipp. At the numerical center of the book (pp. 114-16), Edwin is fleeing from the imposing social figure of Messalina and is forced to use the back stairs which lead him past the hotel's female cleaning staff, which he interprets as a kind of Ur-realm of women reminiscent of Faust's journey toward heaven. Edwin finally confronts a figure which he recognizes as his *Doppelgänger*, but later decides is not even vaguely similar to him. He does, however, realize that the man must be an author and that any resemblance must be due to that fact. The man is Philipp. In traditional folk literature, to meet one's double is an augury of impending death—which Edwin will in fact face as he is attacked by a band of boys as the novel ends. Edwin's initial vision is, however, more accurate than he thought. Philipp indeed represents Edwin's spiritual if not physical double. Both poets have little to offer the war-torn generation of which they are a part. They both realize that they are at a cultural disjunction, at the "Bruchstelle" not only of East and West Germany but also of past spiritual heritage and future technocracy. Both Edwin and Philipp cling to the past, to the world of meaning and coherent tradition. Both are impotent to change or even to reach their own generation and countrymen. If Philipp is "incapable, cowardly, superfluous" as a German author, Edwin is his American counterpart. The devastation of World War II is not limited to Germany nor to the physical environment; it extends also to America and to men's minds and spirits. The watchman, whom Edwin and Philipp must pass after their encounter, recognizes them as brothers in impotence and labels them both, appropriately, "Do-nothings" (p. 116).

The second set of doubles revolves around Emilia. Her personality is not as easily mirrored as Edwin's, however. Emilia is her own double on one level, as Philipp points out. She is both the good, kind Dr. Jekyll and the brutal, violent Mr. Hyde. But in addition to her own doubling, Emilia is reflected in Messalina and the young Massachusetts school teacher, Kay, to whom Emilia gives her own most cherished family jewelry. Each of these figures mirrors a particular aspect of Emilia's personality. Kay is the innocent naive aspect of Emilia that might have survived had the war not destroyed her secure seclusion in the world of wealth. As Emilia watches Kay trying on jewelry, she thinks, "wie nett sie ist, sie ist sehr nett, sie ist ein wirkliches nettes Mädchen, sie ist das nette Mädchen, das ich vielleicht hätte werden können" (p. 164). ("how nice she is, she is very nice, she is a really nice girl, she is the nice girl whom I perhaps could have become.") Kay represents the freedom that Emilia can never find, the open prairie that opposes the closed, molding walls of her own family mansion. Philipp, too, sees a part of Emilia in Kay, but Kay is an unconstrained, an unburdened Emilia. Kay is the person Emilia might have been had she lived in a different time and place. Messalina is the specter of what Emilia might yet become. As Philipp watches the glued waves of Messalina's hair always threatening to engulf him, and the social facade that makes her a mere "monument of a lady," he fears for the sham social creature that Emilia might yet become.

Like Edwin and Philipp, Kay and Emilia, the final pair of doubles is another American-German set. Ezra, the young American whose German mother has filled his imagination with tales of German folklore, and Carla's German son Heinz, who dreams of being an American Indian, engage in their own private combat of eleven-year-old minds. They mirror each other's determination shrewdly to defeat the other in bargaining for a stray dog that runs away before either of them can possess it. The two boys reproduce in miniature the warped impulse to domination that triggered the conflicts of World War II. The fact that the two boys are so alike and that the object of their battle is so absurd only makes their struggle and the larger conflict it mirrors more disturbing. As the future generation, the two boys and their immature battle undercut the hopes of some new world reconciliation. Theirs is a reenactment of the Jewish-Aryan, American-German conflict of the war and a concretization of the struggle and hatred between wealthy and poor that the war left in its wake. The psychological contest of the two boys finally deteriorates to a physical battle amid the ruins of the bombed city. The reality of the physical fight and the near burial of the two boys as a floor collapses under them puts an end to the imaginary gigantic proportions of the conflict. The two end up helping each other out of the rubble and returning to their respective parents. In this final action, the two boys represent, perhaps, Koeppen's hope that the brutality and destruction of the war may have had some positive effect. Ezra returns to his father, Christopher, who has been helping to defend the black soldiers' club from an angry German mob. And Heinz finally returns to the benevolent dream of his mother, Carla, and Washington Price.

Koeppen's pairing of characters, either in sexual relationships or in psychological doubling, lends his novel at least one aspect of hope. For all the dark minds and ruined buildings, *Tauben im Gras* has a more optimistic undertone than Dos Passos' *Manhattan Transfer*.

VI

One other feature of the construction of the book is worth investigating here: the grouping of the characters. The first to appear are those who inhabit the theatrical world and Alexander's apartment—Alexander, his wife Messalina, her lesbian friend the sculptress Alfreda, and, by coincidence, Susanne. The next major introduction is that of Philipp in the Hotel Zum Lamm where he spent the night to escape Emilia's wrath. These two opening scenes are repeated in the same order as the novel closes. Alexander's apartment is then filled with the depressing remnants of Messalina's party (which recalls the boredom of Edwin's lecture) as people doze, chat or drink themselves into oblivion. Emilia, however, has been added to the cast. She is busily engaged in turning herself back into Mr. Hyde and Xanthippe, thus necessitating Philipp's again spending the night at the Hotel Zum Lamm. Philipp is indeed in the hotel in the penultimate narrative passage. But he is not alone; he has brought the young American Kay with him. Kay's exposure to the degrading reality of the shabby hotel and the gambling casino across the street sobers her. She no longer has romantic visions of German poets. And her dream of the American author Edwin shatters also as she hears his cries for help from the alley below. Kay's final gesture is, ironically, to return Emilia's jewelry in order to help Philipp financially. Emilia's attempt at a free and disinterested act returns to the existence of her and Philipp's tortured relationship.

In the repetition of these two opening, introductory scenes as the novel closes, *Tauben im Gras* comes to a rather depressing full cycle. The world of Alexander and Messalina remains a sham whether it is awakening to a new day or falling asleep as the day ends. Emilia returns to her Hyde personality, all gestures of freedom stifled. Philipp remains in his impotent isolation. Edwin's message is host amid his cries for help. All returns to the degradation from which it had momentarily emerged. Only Washington and Carla, and Herr Behrend and Vlasta escape with their dreams intact.

Midway between these opening passages and their closing echoes, one of the novel's strangest characters, the sleepless chemist Schnakenbach, is introduced. In the book's central passage (number fifty-two of 103 narrative passages), Koeppen evokes memories of the many characters of modern literature who are trapped in a twilight zone of consciousness. Schnakenbach, who took drugs to stay awake and cripple his health badly enough to stay out of the war, receives sleep's retribution in his total inability to stay awake because of his drug habit. He physically sleepwalks through life, paralleling in a literal sense Hermann Broch's "Schlafwandler." Schnakenbach also recalls a figure in Rilke's *Malte* who is forced to take to his bed because he considers too closely the idea of the earth's movements. Schnakenbach is similarly lost in his chemical formulae, his entire world reduced to what Dr.

Behude refers to as "gigantic calculations." In the novel's central passage, then, Koeppen presents a character who embodies a science gone berserk, a man whose world is reduced to abstractions and formulae.

The next time the reader encounters him, Schnakenbach is in the America House library as people begin to assemble for Edwin's talk. Schnakenbach later wanders into the lecture and is mistaken for the technician coming to fix the faulty loud-speaker system. Imagining himself before the chemistry class he had formerly conducted, Schnakenbach utters the almost oracular words which serve both as an introduction to Edwin's lecture and as a warning to both Edwin and his audience: "Schlaft nicht! Wacht auf! Es ist Zeit!" (p. 197). ("Don't sleep! Wake up! It is time!"). The image of the turning point, the crisis, the "Bruchstelle" is revived in Schnakenback's ominous words.

Very near the novel's end, it is Schnakenbach's view of the world which comes to dominate. Being led from Edwin's lecture by Dr. Behude, Schnakenbach is described in terms recalling Gertrude Stein's remark about the *Tauben im Gras*: "Sein armer Kopf sah wie ein gerupftes Vogelhaupt aus" (p. 230). ("His poor head looked like a plucked bird-head.") Schnakenback is indeed one of life's pigeons. But his explanation of existence is as coherent as anyone's:

> Eine Unendlichkeit! Aber eine Unendlichkeit zusammengefügt aus allerkleinsten Endlichkeiten, das ist die Welt. Unser Körper, unsere Gestalt, das, von dem wir denken, daß wir es sind, das sind nur lauter Pünktchen, kleine allerallerkleinste Pünktchen. Aber die Pünktchen, die haben es in sich: das sind Kraftstationen, allerallerkleinste Kraftstationen von allergrößter Kraft. Alles kann explodieren! Aber die Milliarden Kraftstationen sind für den kleinsten Augenblick, für unser Leben, wie Sand in dieser Form geweht, die wir unser Ich nennen. Ich könnte Ihnen die Formel aufzeichnen (pp. 229-30).

> An eternity! But an eternity pieced together of the tiniest pieces of finiteness, that is the world. Our body, our form, that of which we think that it is we, these are only little points, little ever so tiny points. But the points, they are the catch: they are power stations, ever so small power stations of the greatest power. Everything can explode! But the billions of power stations are for the briefest moment, for our lifetime, as sand poured into this form which we call our self. I could sketch the formula for you.

The more rational Dr. Behude, who at first thinks Schnakenbach's explanation is nonsense, is forced to admit that it is as plausible as any since man no longer knows himself either microscopically or macroscopically. Behude realizes that Edwin's talk was, ultimately, no more enlightening than Schnakenbach's ramblings.

The reader is left at the novel's close, then, with the rather depressing prospect of meaninglessness on a scientific, cultural, and personal level. The recurrent meaninglessness of the everyday lives of Alexander and Messalina, of Emilia and Philipp, and the idiosyncratic meaninglessness of Schnakenbach's and Edwin's existence fuse to form the newspaper headlines of the modern world and the skeletal structure of the modern novel. *Tauben im Gras* begins, is centered, and ends in that existential emptiness. Its very construction makes the crisis inescapable. But that crisis is also counterbalanced somewhat by juxtaposition with small individual triumphs and ideals. Washington and Carla and their dreams survive. Ezra and Heinz learn something of reality. Kay gains maturity. Herr Behrend and Vlasta remain happy. Cultures, races, nations are successfully fused in some individual lives. The darkness and despair that frame the novel and create its center of gravity are tempered by the small personal successes of a few of the characters. The structural counterbalancing of the novel, built upon the juxtaposition of patterns of hope and of despair, reinforces this basic thematic concern.

VII

Koeppen, then, shares a number of structural principles with Dos Passos. He employs a repetition that runs across the lives of the characters and forms a background of desperation. He depicts self-involvement and disillusionment in many discrete lives. His characters ensnare themselves in their past memories and impale themselves on present realities. But Koeppen, unlike Dos Passos, also provides a pattern of survival in the repetition of individual stories of personal success. His pessimistic reality is not ineluctable. Those characters who can free themselves from their past, sunder national and social ties, and abandon inherited bigotry, can survive. Beside the pattern of despair lies a troubled but still possible pattern of hope. The real tensions of the novel are generated between these two structural components, the two conflicting possibilities as embodied in the lives of individual characters and in their many personal stories in juxtaposition. Koeppen would like to sympathize with Edwin's refutation of the Stein quote which provides the novel's title; he would like to live in "Washington's Inn." But like his countryman Döblin almost a quarter of a century earlier, Koeppen has seen too much of modern, urban, military reality and its devastation to present an easy solution of optimism. Unlike Döblin, however, Koeppen lets reality get the better of his ideal; he lets the harsh, meaningless side of existence provide the dominant framework.

One may still wonder, however, why Koeppen's novel resembles Dos Passos' *Manhattan Transfer* so strikingly. There are, of course, several possible explanations. We know that Koeppen greatly valued Dos Passos' works and was probably strongly influenced by them.[10] On the other hand, he also knows the works of Joyce and Döblin. Influence alone, then, does not provide a sufficient explanation. It could as well have created a structure resembling Joyce's *Ulysses* as one resembling Dos Passos' work.

A more compelling factor in producing the structural similarities between *Manhattan Transfer* and *Tauben im Gras* are the parallel cultural crises during which the two novels came into existence. Dos Passos' novel was written shortly after World War I. Section III of the book specifically depicts the postwar era. Dos Passos was writing at a time of social turmoil, historical upheaval, and cultural fragmentation. The economic situation was deteriorating; the poor and destitute among the urban population were becoming more evident. Fortunes collapsed; men rose or fell on the social ladder; cultural and social traditions disappeared. In this sense the American city which Dos Passos observed was similar to the German city which Koeppen examines. *Tauben im Gras*, too, is written immediately after a war, World War II. Germany is also at the point of economic and social crisis. The old order is being transposed into an as yet indiscernible new order. Koeppen's Germany is at a "Bruchstelle" both politically and culturally just as was Dos Passos' America a quarter of a century earlier.

I would argue that the similar cultural stages of Dos Passos' America in 1925 and Koeppen's Germany in 1951 produce a number of similar cultural problems and imperatives for the two authors. The pressures produced by the similar situations may well have induced Dos Passos and Koeppen to create structurally similar correlatives of their experience. This is not to suggest that the literary structures merely imitate cultural structures but rather that an exchange takes place between literature and its cultural context, an exchange in which observation of a disorienting cultural situation and creative resistance to it interact to generate the literary text.

The historical situations of Dos Passos and Koeppen are certainly not exactly the same. America may have been in turmoil after World War I, but it did emerge on the victorious side. Germany after World War II, on the other hand, still lay in the ruins of a devastating defeat. But the two authors share a feeling of cultural rupture, of a crisis that tore them away from earlier cultural traditions and left them floating in a world of meaningless repetition. Both authors are at a cultural "Bruchstelle" that engulfs their characters, too, in a sea of change with no apparent retaining walls. Both authors feel compelled to record the fragmented quality of the reality which surrounds them. But both authors also feel the need to simplify even that chaotic fragmentation by creating repetitions of basic human situations.

Dos Passos and Koeppen do not have the critical distance to point up the ironic differences between modern civilization and earlier cultural archetypes as Döblin does constantly in *Berlin Alexanderplatz*. It is painfully evident to Dos Passos and Koeppen that their worlds consist of the repetition of inescapable human events in fragmented isolation. Their novels both acknowledge that chaos and attempt to impose some sort of simplifying aesthetic order on it. In this last respect, Koeppen varies Dos Passos' simple multilinear structure somewhat by providing a consistent pattern of hope in opposition to that of meaningless reiteration of events. Both authors resort to the basic, relatively straightforward multilinearity of plots in an attempt to provide some order and coherence in a world of postwar confusion and cultural upheaval.

VI
Conclusion

FOLLOWING THE EXAMINATION of four multilinear novels, some conclusions can be made—about the books individually, about multilinear novels in general, and about the efficacy of the method employed in this study. We should consider, further, what the use of a fragmentary, multilinear structure implies about the author, the narrator, and the problem of the demise of the omniscient narrator in modern narrative texts.

First, the method of considering the multilinear novels on a cross-cultural basis allows the texts to illuminate one another. Common literary techniques and similarities of historical perspective begin to elucidate generic characteristics. The very fact of a concentration of such novels in a particular period suggests a common cultural motivation for the works. And eventually the understanding of each individual text is facilitated by a comprehension of the group as a whole.

Considering the individual texts on the most elementary level, we have found that each of the novels examined has one or several basic structuring principles which generate the surface architecture of the work. In Faulkner's *As I Lay Dying*, the structuring components are two symmetrical patterns, one of the fulfillment of a mythic plot and the other of a range of human consciousness as presented in the multiple narrators. These two form the basic axes of the novel's structure and generate the comic and tragic tensions that torment the Bundren Family. In Döblin's *Berlin Alexanderplatz*, the central plot line of Franz Biberkopf's personal trials and development is paralleled and elucidated in biblical and literary allusions, while a structural dissonance is created by the conflicting uses of interpolated narratives and documentary materials. The surface structure of Dos Passos' *Manhattan Transfer* is generated primarily by a principle of repetition of specific passages, incidents and images across the lives of many characters and across the text as a whole. And finally, Koeppen in his *Tauben im Gras* counterbalances the darker repetition of entrapment, disillusion, and despair with the repeated life patterns of couples who succeed in personal, social, racial, and cultural reconciliations.

The structural complexity of these works ranges from an elegantly economical structure in the two-dimensional narrative matrix of Faulkner's novel to the multidimensional and highly complex surface arrangement of Döblin's syncopated orchestration of many techniques. Dos Passos' and Koeppen's books represent simpler structures. Dos Passos repeats and varies a basic dilemma in each of the three sections of his novel. Koeppen creates somewhat more complexity by stubbornly maintaining a pattern of possible hope against the seemingly inescapable pattern of despair in postwar Munich.

These comments on structuring principles and structural complexity do not, of course, imply anything about the philosophical or psychological depth of the individual novels or about their literary quality. Structural complexity alone does not ensure a corresponding philosophical complexity or literary value. (The structurally "simplest" of the four novels, namely Faulkner's *As I Lay Dying*, may well be the "best" in terms of literary and philosophical value.) The investigation of embedded structures has given us tools of analysis rather than a yardstick for critical evaluation. After coming to understand how a particular text is constructed and what causes its architecture and dynamic tensions, we must still make the critical leap of evaluating quality from our own personal criteria. But having gained tools of analysis is no mean accomplishment, particularly in the case of such initially inaccessible texts as those multilinear novels we have examined. Such tools help us to understand the correspondences between structure and theme, form and content, and technique and meaning in each work. They aid us in comprehending the literary piece, a prerequisite to any evaluation of quality.

Have we, however, learned anything beyond the structural principles of each individual text? Can we now extrapolate from the four novels more general statements of what the novels share in terms of themes and techniques, and of what problems multilinear texts in general create for the reader and critic? I am interested here in using the structural insights we have gained to aid in understanding the larger literary dilemmas that generated them and to achieve a more complete comprehension of the texts in their literary and historical contexts. The question becomes, then, what do these texts share in the realms of theme, technique, and structure? What do they have in common that might allow us to draw more general conclusions?

They all have, most obviously, a fragmented literary surface in which discrete narrative passages are juxtaposed without logical transitions or explanations. Coupled with this, the books create a difficulty for the reader by calling into question the narrator's dependability. Faulkner's *As I Lay Dying* has fifteen different narrators with no overriding omniscient or even organizing voice within the dramatic framework of the novel. Döblin's *Berlin Alexanderplatz* features a rather Shandian narrator whose intellectual meanderings range from considerations of the age of the sun to comparisons of chickens, but who in himself provides no dependable guidance for the reader. Dos Passos' *Manhattan Transfer* has a narrative voice which is often eloquently lyrical in the introductory passages to each chapter, but which offers no solutions, no alternatives for interpreting the recurrent events of the novel, and which is itself drawn into the book's ineluctable repetitions. Koeppen's *Tauben im Gras* also possesses an identifiable narrative voice which at times becomes emotionally involved in events but which presents no more salient or authoritative explanations than Edwin or Schnakenbach do. All four novels, then, retain narrators but do not give them a guiding role. The narrator becomes another facet of the multilinear narrative surface, adding to rather than easing the complexities of interpretation.

The four novels also share a number of narrative techniques. The use of extra-literary, documentary material to evoke a particular historical background is common to Döblin's, Dos Passos' and Koeppen's work as is the use of popular songs and biblical allusions. (Faulkner's other novels such as *The Sound and the Fury* and *Absalom, Absalom!* also share these techniques.) All four novels use a constant shift in focus from the mind of one character to that of another, a shift usually motivated by the characters' participation in the same activity (as in *As I Lay Dying* and *Manhattan Transfer*) or linked by verbal repetitions (as in *Tauben im Gras* and *Berlin Alexanderplatz*).

All four books also depict the workings of a society, on a larger or smaller scale, and the effects of those social systems on the individuals within them. This is readily apparent in the socially oriented, urban novels of Döblin, Dos Passos, and Koeppen; but even Faulkner's novel is interested in the interactions within the Bundren Family as a social unit and between the family and the larger society. Faulkner's focus, in fact, becomes just that struggle of the individual consciousness against the momentum of the social unit to restore its equilibrium. And in each book the individual conflicts of discrete characters are generalized into larger conflicts by allusions, repetitions, and juxtapositions. The embedded structures in the books thus offer larger social comments than are readily discernible in the surface of the texts. This basic tension between the individual and larger social or cultural forces becomes central to each of the novels.

These last characteristics (i.e., the use of extra-literary, documentary material and the concern with depicting the complexities of a social milieu) firmly connect the formally innovative multilinear texts to the more traditional socio-historical concerns of the novel throughout its development. The closeness of Dos Passos' novel to earlier nineteenth-century novels in the realistic and naturalistic tradition has been pointed out by a number of critics. But the novels of Döblin, Faulkner, and Koeppen also participate in those traditions through their interest in the social factors that interact with individual lives. The difference between these multi-linear texts and their realistic and naturalistic predecessors is the complexity of the factors involved. The simpler self-evident correspondences between man's internal world and his public actions and institutions has given way to a more obscure system of interactions. The causality linking environment and individual development confidently assumed by the naturalist novelist is replaced in the multilinear novel by a welter of possible external influences that may or may not be assimilated by the individual.

The focus of the multilinear novels, then, is still man and his society, but the precise interactions between the two have become much more difficult to discern and depict. The twentieth-century novelist, no longer willing or philosophically able to adopt the omniscient stance, chooses the more indirect methods of embedded forms, juxtapositions and repetitions of events, and allusion to force the reader to participate in his more equivocal comments on the position of the individual in the modern world. Ironically, the structural and formal idiosyncrasies of these multilinear novels do not exile them from the traditional realms of novelistic interest but become new tools for expressing and investigating the progress of the individual's understanding and development in relation to his society.

The factor that is new in the multilinear novelists' writing is their placing a greater burden of interpretation on the reader. Since author and reader no longer share an assumed system of "truth" about the world in which they live, the two must work together to build a system of meaning and understanding. By selection, juxtaposition and structuring, the twentieth-century novelist creates a fictional world which presents some of the complexity and uncertainty of his experienced world. The reader, in turn, must enter into the fictional world and work to discover for himself the underlying systems of order deeply embedded within it. The process of reading the multilinear text, then, is a correlative of "reading" one's world in general. The formal and structural experimentation in these novels constantly forces the individual to search for deeper systems of meaning within an apparently chaotic group of perceptions just as he must do in his externally experienced world. It is not so much that any one technique or group of techniques simply imitates the modern world at large but rather that the formal experimentation demands from the reader a process of individual interpretation similar to that needed to survive the modern experience. Formal experimentation thus participates in the renewal and revision of its cultural context while it is influenced by it.

In addition to the struggle between individual consciousness and some larger controlling force, the four texts share more specific features such as types of characters, and tragic or comic tone. Again the two novels most separated in time show the closest similarities of character types. Dos Passos and Koeppen create a number of characters at one stage or another of social prominence. Both authors focus a good part of their attention on a writer figure—Dos Passos selects Jimmy Herf, and Koeppen uses Philipp. And both Herf and Philipp fail to create lasting works, to reach their contemporaries with their most profound messages and to adjust to the urban reality that surrounds them. Koeppen and Dos Passos also create a female partner for their writers in the characters of Emilia and Ellen. These women search continually for happiness and security, and both fail to find it because they are tied to dead dreams and memories. The generative power of woman and the generative power of the artist are both stifled by a failure to create or locate those deeper systems of shared meaning that the multilinear novelists themselves are seeking to create.

Faulkner and Döblin also have certain types of characters in common. Focusing largely on uneducated social groups—the Bundren Family and the Berlin underworld—they deal with a number of characters of limited intellectual ability, most notably Anse and Franz Biberkopf. Perhaps the very limitation of intellectual capacity intensifies the struggle of the characters with larger controlling forces they cannot comprehend. Faulkner, however, balances the limited characters with the all-enveloping consciousness of Addie and Darl, who envision the larger pattern. The narrator in Döblin's novel serves this function by outlining Franz's story in advance, by providing "Bänkelgesang" commentary, and by juxtaposing enlightening allusions to Franz's story. In both cases, however, the connection of the man of limited intelligence with more primal forces of vitality and survival comments, to some extent, on the dangers of solipsism and impotence which haunt the more perceptive and sensitive characters in all four books.

The four novels, then, have several character types in common. But in comparing them, the factor of central importance is the struggle of all these character types with larger, uncontrollable systems of meaning. Yet we are not justified in viewing the books as tragic conflicts between the individual and a larger fate—at least not without qualifications. Döblin goes out of his way in *Berlin Alexanderplatz* to undercut the whole idea of fate, of fated tragedies in life. The pattern to which Franz must accommodate himself is an entirely human one generated by the practical functioning of human beings in societies and not designed by some greater romantic or Greek powers. The God to whom Franz must answer is one who demands only human cooperation and responsibility. Dos Passos and Koeppen, likewise, create entirely anthropocentric systems of meaning. Men destroy themselves and one another; they are not destroyed by the fateful hand of unseen gods. The inability of characters to comprehend and control the larger patterns of meaning does not, in itself, make their conflicts tragic. These novels lack the very concept of fate in the classical sense, necessary to true tragedy. What had been a personalized struggle of the individual with the powers that control the world, becomes for these modern authors of urban reality what Sartre terms "a statistical determinism."[1] Sartre goes on to describe this modern replacement for fate in his essay on Dos Passos:

> [Dos Passos' characters], submerged in their own existences, live as they can. They struggle; what comes their way is not determined in advance. And yet, neither their efforts, their faults, nor their most extreme violence can interfere with the regularity of births, marriages and suicides. The pressure exerted by a gas on the walls of its container does not depend upon the individual histories of the molecules composing it.[2]

In the modern world, fate becomes statistical determinism, and men become very much like molecules of gas in a huge urban container—at least for Dos Passos and Koeppen, and, more strugglingly, for Döblin. The personalized conflict of the individual with the larger controlling forces of the world breaks up into an impersonal struggle for survival. That is, partly, what creates the impulse to multilinear fragmentation. No longer able to envision a controlling system of meaning outside of himself, the author is forced to create a multifarious, fragmented system of his own. However, at the same time as he depicts the chaotic and fragmentary dilemma of characters in a modern world, the author himself can suggest an aesthetic order on a deeper level by providing a more coherent embedded structure in his text. The author can succeed in perceiving and manipulating in his text those deeper patterns of meaning which his characters frequently cannot reach.

I have so far avoided discussing Faulkner's *As I Lay Dying* in the context of fate and tragedy. Of all four authors, Faulkner comes closest to creating a really tragic work. The reason, I think, is that he manages to tie the humanly generated conflicts of the Bundren Family's journey to an earlier pattern of myth and fate. Certainly Döblin with his biblical allusions and Koeppen with his classical names attempt a similar linking. But Döblin and Koeppen only allude. They return always to the human, social plane of their narrative where such systems have long since given way to fragmented urban activity. Faulkner, on the other hand, in *As I Lay Dying* refrains from the classical and biblical allusions so frequent in his other novels. He chooses, rather, to incorporate the older systems of myth and fate into the very structure of his novel. The idea of a personal struggle of each of his characters to align his individual destiny with a larger pattern of meaning is still very much alive in *As I Lay Dying*. The Bundren Family presents a more coherently human social unit than Manhattan, Munich, or Berlin. The family is still linked to the earth and to the primal powers of fire and flood. And the family members are still closely tied to one another, to primitive tradition, and to ritual. Faulkner's world has not yet yielded to "statistical determinism." His human individuals are struggling with a pattern much older than themselves, which has gained a cultural momentum that eventually engulfs them all. Only their conflict, of all those in the four novels we examined, has the potential to be a tragic one.

The conflict is tragic, however, only for those characters who can envision, if not comprehend, its scope—that is, for Addie and Darl. And even Addie is excluded from the tragic struggle by her departure before the central conflict begins. That leaves only Darl, who forfeits his position as a tragic hero by continually attempting to halt or disrupt the mythic pattern. Darl seeks escape, not tragic heroism, and he finally attains it in his insanity. That clears our potentially tragic stage of everyone but Anse, the real hero of the tale. And with Anse, we move not only from tragedy to comedy (by virtue of Anse's success in the novel) but to parody. The hero has descended to the figure of the toothless, hunchbacked, selfish old farmer spitting clichés into the dust and frustrating every thinking human being within miles. The potential tragic impulse in Faulkner's novel ends in parody—as do so many of the attempts to link modern reality to an older, more comprehensive and consistent system of meaning. Our modern tragedy is frequently not one of fateful conflict but of alienation from any tradition powerful enough to generate such a conflict. Koeppen's Philipp and Edwin realize this, as do Döblin's narrator and Dos Passos himself.

In each novel, then, the individual characters' lives are acted upon by larger patterns of events which the characters do not create and cannot control. The authors give up omniscience but take on god-like powers of manipulation of reality by selection, juxtaposition, and repetition. It is no longer the characters' own life stories that constitute the plot. The "plot" becomes a larger conflict, a struggle between those individual lives and the greater patterns of myth (in Faulkner), society (in Dos Passos and Döblin) and history (in Koeppen) which affect them.

Where do those larger patterns come from? They cannot be consciously generated by the characters, who are often unaware of them. The larger patterns generally run across the lives of many characters, involving them in interpersonal struggles. It would also be difficult for the narrators alone to be responsible for the larger patterns since they are often caught themselves in those patterns (as with Faulkner's fifteen narrators or Döblin's narrator) and since the patterns frequently run across comments provided by the narrator and those provided by individual characters (especially in Dos Passos' work where passages move verbatim from narrator to character). The larger patterns must come, then, from the selective perception of the author. No longer willing to claim omniscience through the narrator, the author still maintains complete control by presenting only carefully culled sections of the reality he is depicting. Ironically, those authors who apparently present a cross section, a representative sampling of a particular environment (i.e., Dos Passos and Koeppen) must, because of the very scope of their undertaking, be most selective. And they tend, of course, to select examples which buttress their main themes, incidents which repeat their central message. This type of authorial control is, in fact, more difficult to escape or refute than the old-fashioned omniscient narrator since it is harder to identify. The authors who felt uncomfortable sharing with God the intellectual and moral burdens of omniscience have instead replaced Him completely by authorial manipulations built into the very structure of their works. We end up, in a sense, with a much more personally biased view of the world than we had with the morally self-righteous omniscient narrators. The fragmented, structurally complex multilinear novel represents a highly artificial aesthetic whole of selective bits of reality cemented together by the controlling consciousness of the author.

The aim of the method I have employed—the construction and analysis of narrative matrices and the relating of thematic material to the structural surface—is to identify the principles of that authorial selectivity in each individual work. In Faulkner's *As I Lay Dying* we discovered that individual consciousness and mythic pattern were the primary structuring components. In Döblin's *Berlin Alexanderplatz* the underlying principle could be identified as individual development versus interpersonal responsibility as revealed through techniques such as biblical and literary allusions, interpolated narratives and documentary materials. In Dos Passos' *Manhattan Transfer* inescapable repetition of incidents and images structured the work. And in Koeppen's *Tauben im Gras* desperate repetition was tempered by a repeated pattern of personal reconciliation of disparate racial, social and cultural elements.

Without constructing precise matrices or analyzing structures we would still be unsure as to where and how the themes interact. We would be hard put, for example, to discern the carefully symmetrical construction of *As I Lay Dying* and the effect of its two conflicting patterns of symmetry. We might well have missed the important parallels in the lives of Bud, Stan, and Anna—all secondary characters—and their function of ineluctable repetition without having noticed their parallel structural positions. And to what extent would we recognize the thematic reinforcement of Franz Biberkopf's development by the biblical and literary allusions without having seen the structural reinforcements? The matrices and the analysis of structures serve to jog our literary intuition, to sharpen the vague outlines and notions of the books in our minds, to increase our sensitivity to the individual text. They help us to keep in mind and in view the entire novel so that we can follow a theme, technique, or image across a large work just as we would in analyzing a short lyric poem, to see in more detail the underlying generating principles of the text.

The four books taken chronologically represent a basic generic type, two variations on that model, and a return again to the basic multilinear type. Dos Passos' *Manhattan Transfer*, the earliest example, provides the simplest form of the multilinear genre. It consists of a number of parallel plot lines related by repetition. Döblin greatly expands the idea of multilinearity by increasing the narrative voices rather than merely the number of separate plots. Faulkner, too, creates a multilinear variation by multiplying the actual number of narrators within the dramatic framework of the novel's action. And, finally, Koeppen's *Tauben im Gras* represents a return to the earlier simple form displayed in *Manhattan Transfer*. The genre, then, begins with a basic version of the multi-linear novel, goes through several variations and complications, and finally returns to the simpler form under the pressure of social and cultural dissolution.

There remains, of course, an enormous number of multilinear texts to be studied. A look back in literary history would reveal earlier novels with an impulse in the direction of fragmentation and multilinearity such as *Trimstram Shandy* or *Jacques le fataliste*. These forerunners of the twentieth-century multilinear genre would deepen our understanding of both the general characteristics of the sub-genre and the importance of cultural context in generating it. A look aside to other early twentieth-century examples of the genre such as Aldous Huxley's *Point Counter Point* or Hermann Broch's *Die Schlafwandler* would further extend our understanding as would a look forward in time to more recent examples such as Josef Heller's *Catch 22* or Heinrich Böll's *Gruppenbild mit Dame*. The study of the French tradition from Gide's *Les Faux-monnayeurs* to the *nouveau roman* writers would also be an appropriate parallel to our study. Such additional research will allow more concrete analysis of the development and history of this literary sub-genre as well as of its manifestations in varying cultural and historical situations. The aim of the present study is to serve as an impetus to such further research and to provide a possible method for conducting it.

One question, however, still remains to be answered. Why does this particular narrative genre become so prominent during the Twentieth Century? Why do so many modern authors show an affinity for this fragmented, multilinear structure? Koeppen actually answered this question rather concisely in a phrase I quoted earlier: "Dieser Stil entspricht unserem Empfinden, unserem Bewußtsein, unserer bitterer Erfahrung." ("This style corresponds to our sensation, our consciousness, our bitter experience.") Our modern world, made up of myriad social, technological, and political facets, preserving the shards of earlier cultures from which it is forever alienated, threatening always to return to total dissociation, no longer lends itself to the comfortable concensus necessary to the omniscient stance adopted by novelists of earlier centuries. Modern writers are forced to wrestle with a complex environment that recalcitrantly refuses to yield up a consistent and obvious public meaning. The modern author must use the confusing raw material of sensation to construct his own system of meaning. When Koeppen states that the multilinear style corresponds to our experience, he is not merely suggesting that individual techniques reflect specific aspects of the external world or that the overall structure of the text simply reflects modern chaos. He implies rather that the method of constructing a modern text participates in the same effort to interpret sensation and to generate individual systems of meaning which modern man is constantly forced to engage in in his everyday struggle to survive.

Having experienced the philosophical upheaval created by the works of Einstein, Bergson, Freud and others, and faced with the unavoidable relativity of modern science, morality, and consciousness itself, the modern writer is forced to confront a world without common ordering principles. He must, therefore, provide a subjective system of order within the text itself and communicate that system to his reader in a way that allows them to share a process of perceiving meaning commonly in an otherwise disjointed world. The characteristics of those individual systems of order will be as various as the works themselves. They may entail a multiplication of points-of-view or of plot lines, or they may incorporate older systems of order through allusion and quotation. In each case, however, the author faces the problem of creating common meaning in a world which supplies none itself. The creation of that meaning takes place not in a definitive statement by an omniscient author to his reader, but rather in the common process by which they come to share a subjectively perceived sense of a system of order within a larger chaotic picture.

The act of creating a text and of perceiving the underlying system of meaning in that text becomes a joint effort by the author and his reader in the battle against the solipsism that constantly threatens to engulf them both. The process is a "bitter experience" because it is an inescapable and relentless pressure on modern man to create his own meaning and then to attempt to share it. The effort of the multilinear novelists becomes a model for this process. And they contribute, in their turn, to a new set of conventions for a modern system of meaning based not on the shared public faith of earlier generations but rather on a shared group of aesthetic experiences and on the shared capacity to perceive meaning in those experiences. The modern novelist, then, is faced with the paradoxical challenge of acknowledging and conveying the impact of his dissociated world while at the same time writing against its total dissolution by imposing his selective aesthetic order upon the chaos of modern experience.

Appendix I

Manhattan Transfer

THE FOLLOWING THREE diagrams form a narrative matrix for Dos Passos' *Manhattan Transfer*. The order of appearance of the various characters is displayed on the horizontal axis while the order of the chapters and their smaller subdivisions are charted on the vertical axis. Because of the length of the original matrix, each of the novel's major sections was given its own diagram. The characters' names have also been abbreviated according to the key given below. A character's name appearing in parenthesis indicates that the character has either died or been undone at that point. The "xx" listing indicates a character who only appears once in the novel.

SECTION I:

El—Ellen	PS—Phil Sandbourne
Bu—Bud	ME—Mr. Emery
ET—Ed Thatcher	EM—Emily Merivale
ST—Susie Thatcher	JM—Jeff Merivale
Em—Emile	PB—Phineas P. Blackhead
Co—Congo	MM—Maisie Merivale
GM—Gus McNiel	JM—James Merivale
GB—George Baldwin	JH—Joe Harland
MR—Mmr. Rigaud	JO—Jojo Oglethorpe
Ji—Jimmy Herf	CM—Cpt. McAvoy
MH—Mrs. Herf	NM—Nellie McNiel

SECTION II:

(newly introduced characters)

Ru—Ruth
Ca—Cassandra
St—Stan
Go—Goldweiser
CB—Ceciley Baldwin
Jo—Joe O'Keefe
To—Tony
Bu—Bullock
Pe—Pearline Emery
MS—Martin Schiff

SECTION III:

(newly introduced characters)

An—Anna
AM—Anna's mother
MH—Martin Herf
Hi—Frances and Bob Hildebrand
DR—Dutch Robertson
De—Densch
Fr—Francie
JR—Jake and Rosie Silverman
Ne—Nevada
RA—Roy and Alice
MC—Mrs. Jack Cunningham
El.—Elmer
JC—Jack Cunningham

MANHATTAN TRANSFER: SECTION I

		El	Bu	ET	ST	xx	Em Co	GM	GB	NM	MR	Ji	MH	EM	JM	PS	ME
I Ferryslip	1	El															
	2		Bu														
	3	El		ET	ST												
	4					xx											
II Metropolis	5			ET													
	6					xx											
	7		Bu														
	8	El		ET	ST												
	9					xx											
	10						Em Co										
	11	El		ET	ST												
	12					xx											
	13		Bu			xx											
	14					xx	Em Co										
	15					xx											
	16		Bu		ST												
	17	El															
	18				ST			GM									
III Dollars	19	El															
	20								GB								
	21								GB	NM							
	22						Em Co				MR						
	23		Bu			xx											
	24					xx											
	25	El		ET				GM	GB	NM		Ji					
	26		Bu										MH				
	27													EM	JM		
	28							GM		NM						PS	
	29					xx											ME

CONTINUED

30										
31		Em		NM	Ji	MH	EM			
32	Bu		GB							
33		xx						PB		
34									MM JM JH	
35		Em Co			Ji		EM JM			
36	ET									
37										
38		Em		MR	Ji (MH)					
39		xx			Ji		EM JM			
40	El									JO
41		xx			Ji		JM			
42	(Bu)									CM

IV — Tracks

V — Steamroller

MANHATTAN TRANSFER: SECTION I

MANHATTAN TRANSFER: SECTION II

	No.	El	Ji	JO	Ru	Ca	GB	St	JH	xx	Mc	PS	Go	CB	Jo	ET	GM	NM	To	Co	Bu
I Lady on WH	43	El	Ji	JO	Ru	Ca															
	44	El		JO			GB	St													
II Longlegged Jack of the Isthmus	45	El						St	JH												
	46	El						St		xx											
	47	El	Ji																		
	48	El			Ru																
	49					Ca			JH	xx	Mc										
	50					Ca															
	51	El																			
III Nine Days' Wonder	52	El								xx		PS									
	53	El	Ji	JO				St													
	54								JH	xx											
	55	El					GB						Go								
	56													CB							
	57	El				Ca			JH												
	58	El													Jo						
	59	El	Ji	JO			GB	St													
	60	El								xx						ET					
IV Fire Engine	61	El					GB						Go								
	62	El						St	JH	xx					Jo		GM				
	63	El						St		xx			Go								
V Went to Animal's Fair	64	El	Ji				GB										GM	NM	To	Co	Bu
	65	El	Ji				GB													Co	Bu
	66	El					GB														
	67	El	Ji				GB								Jo		GM	NM	To	Co	Bu
	68	El	Ji				GB								Jo						Bu

CONTINUED

VI	Five Stat. Quest.	69	El				
		70	El	JH xx	Jo		Pe
		71	El	St xx	Go		
		72	Ji	JH			
VII	Roller Coaster	73	(St)	St xx	GM		Pe
		74					
		75					
VIII	One m. River to Jordan	76	El	Ru Ca	GB	PS	
		77	El				
		78	El	Ji	xx	Go	
		79	El		xx		
		80	El	(aborts [St's] baby)			
		81	El			MS	

MANHATTAN TRANSFER: SECTION II

MANHATTAN TRANSFER: SECTION III

Line	Entries (left → right)
82	EM MM JM
83	xx An AM
84	El Ji MH HI
85	GB
86	Jo DR
87	EM MM JM El Ji Jo
88	xx GB
89	GB GM De
90	xx
91	xx El Ji DR Ru
92	Fr
93	An Co
94	
95	EM MM JM JR
96	GB GM
97	An To Ne
98	GM
99	Jo DR
100	
101	Ji Hi
102	EM JM xx GB De Co RA
103	
104	El Ji MH MC
105	An
106	GB Ru Ca To Ne
107	JM GB JO
108	El Ji PB El.
109	NM
110	An
111	JC (JR)

I Rejoicing / City that / Dwelt Carelessly

II Nickel-odeon

III Revolving Doors

CONTINUED

MANHATTAN TRANSFER: SECTION III

IV — Skyscraper

Page	xx	An	AM	El	Ji	DR	De	Fr	RA	El.	MS
112					Ji						
113		An			Ji	DR		Fr			
114			AM						RA	El.	MS
115											
116					Ji	DR		Fr			
117							De				
118					Ji						
119	xx			El							
120	xx			El							
121	xx				Ji						

V — The Burthen of Nineveh

Page	JM	xx	An	El	Ji	Hi	MH	GB	DR	De	Co	Em	Fr	Ne	RA	MC	PB
122										De							
123				El			MH										
124				El				GB									
125		xx															
126															RA		
127		xx			Ji												
128											Co	Em		Ne			
129	JM																
130		xx	An														
131		xx	An														
132																MC	
133									(DR)				(Fr)				
134																	(PB)
135		xx	(An)	El													
136		xx		El	Ji	Hi											

Appendix II
Berlin Alexanderplatz

THE FOLLOWING THREE charts record the structural interaction of various literary techniques and the main plot line of Franz Biberkopf's development. Figure I reveals a corresponding structural arrangement in the use of biblical allusions and the development of Franz. Figure II shows that the literary allusions also have clear structural divisions but that these do not correspond to the main structural divisions in Franz's life. And finally, Figure III displays the lack of any discernible structural divisions among the interpolated narratives. The three figures taken in sequence, then, would form an increasingly complex structural arrangement in which the main plot line is at first reinforced and then obscured as new techniques are added.

FIGURE I
REINFORCING STRUCTURAL PATTERNS

Books

	1	2	3	4	5	6	7	8	9
Books 1	FB out of *prison* Jerem.	*Adam & Eve* naive garden	Snake in garden	Eccles. *Job*	Jeremiah	Whore of Babyl. *Abrah. & Isaac*	*Abrah. & Isaac*	Eccles. (Seine Zeit) Revela. whore	Revela. whore Eccles. (two together)
Books 2	FB gets footing in Berlin	Adam & Eve story reinforces FB's naive betrayal by his friend Lüders							
Books 3	Lüders betrays FB								
Books 4	FB recovers from first blow			Job's story of over much pride & self-reliance CONTINUED					

← FRANZ BIBERKOPF'S PERSONAL DEVELOPMENT

FRANZ BIBERKOPF'S PERSONAL DEVELOPMENT					BIBLICAL ALLUSIONS →
5 — FB in robbery pushed from car			reinforces FB's arrogance with Reinhold		
6 — FB back from loss of arm sees Reinhold				Isaac's willing self-sacrifice parallels Mieze's self-sacrifice & FB's need to be a willing victim	
7 — Reinhold kills Mieze					
8 — FB learns M. dead, seeks Re. FB arrested					Defeat of whore by death parallels FB's rebirth & Ecclesiastes sets up social reintegration of FB
9 — FB in asylum reborn as new social man					

FIGURE II
THREE-PART PATTERNS BUT SKEWED STRUCTURALLY

Books

	1	2	3	4	5	6	7	8	9
Books 1	FB out of prison of prison	Kleist's *Prinz Friedrich* Aeschylus' *Oresteia*		Homer's *Odyssey*	*Knabens Wunderborn* Es ist e. Schnitter	Es ist ein Schnit.	Es ist ein Schnit.	Es ist ein Schnit.	Dream play of F's life Es ist e. Schnitter
2	FB gets footing in Berlin								
3	Lüders betrays FB								
4	FB recovers from first blow								CONTINUED

FRANZ BIBERKOPF'S PERSONAL DEVELOPMENT ←

FB in robbery pushed from car — 5

FB back from loss of arm sees Reinhold — 6

Reinhold kills Mieze — 7

FB learns M. dead, seeks Re. FB arrested — 8

FB in asylum reborn as new social man — 9

← FRANZ BIBERKOPF'S PERSONAL DEVELOPMENT →

← LITERARY ALLUSIONS →

FIGURE III

DISSONANCE OF TWO AXES — STRUCTURAL COMPLICATION

Books   No Discernable Divisions on this Axis

	1	2	3	4	5	6	7	8	9
1	Zannowich story	Kneipe ruined individual lives	War veteran with dying son	Gerner couple with	Suicide couple	Carpenter's sick family	Finke-Bornemann, Pussi Uhl	Mieze's Life	Mother & seven sons die
1	FB out of prison								
2	FB gets footing in Berlin								
3	Lüders betrays FB								
4	FB recovers from first blow								
5	FB in robbery pushed from car								CONTINUED

Books

← FRANZ BIBERKOPF'S PERSONAL DEVELOPMENT

				INTERPOLATED NARRATIVES ⟶
FB back from loss of arm sees Reinhold				
Reinhold kills Mieze				
FB learns M. dead, seeks Re. FB arrested				
FB in asylum reborn as new social man				

6 ⌣ 7 ⌣ 8 ⌣ 9

FRANZ BIBERKOPF'S PERSONAL DEVELOPMENT ⟶

Appendix III
As I Lay Dying

THE FOLLOWING NARRATIVE matrix displays the order of appearance of the narrators in _As I Lay Dying_ on the horizontal axis while tracing the action as it unfolds on the vertical axis. The vertical axis has been further divided according to the location of the action. Characters' names have been abbreviated according to the key given below.

The names of characters belonging to the Bundren Family are seen in capital letters while those of non-kin narrators have been shown in lower case letters. The top line of the matrix displays the arrangement of the members of the Bundren Family without the presence of the non-kin narrators.

KEY TO ABBREVIATIONS
OF CHARACTERS' NAMES:

DA—Darl

co—Cora

JE—Jewel

DD—Dewey Dell

tu—Tull

AN—Anse

pe—Peabody

VA—Vardaman

CA—Cash

sa—Samson

AD—Addie

wh—Whitfield

ar—Armstid

mo—Moseley

mc—Macgowan

#	DA	JE	DD	AN	VA	CA	AD
Home / Addie Alive							
1	DA						
2	co						
3	DA						
4		JE					
5	DA						
6	co						
7			DD				
8			tu				
9				AN			
10	DA						
11				pe			
12	DA						
Home / Addie Dead							
13					VA		
14			DD				
15					VA		
16			tu				
17	DA						
18						CA	
19					VA		
20			tu				
21	DA						
22						CA	
23	DA						
24					VA		
25	DA						
Road (Earth)							
26				AN			
27	DA						
28				AN			
29						sa	
30			DD				

Group	#	DA	co	DD	tu	pe	VA	CA	AD	wh	ar	mo	mc
River (Water)	31				tu								
	32	DA											
	33				tu								
	34	DA											
	35						VA						
	36				tu								
	37	DA											
	38							CA					
ADDIE	39		co										
	40								AD				
	41									wh			
Road (Earth)	42	DA											
	43										ar		
	44						VA						
	45											mo	
	46	DA											
	47						VA						
	48	DA											
Barn (Fire)	49						VA						
	50	DA											
	51						VA						
Jefferson / Darl Sane	52	DA											
	53							CA					
Jefferson / Darl Insane	54					pe							
	55												mc
	56						VA						
	57	DA											
	58			DD									
	59							CA					

Appendix IV
Tauben im Gras

THE FOLLOWING DIAGRAM reveals the continual criss-crossing of the stories of Philipp, Emilia, Washington, Carla, Herr Behrend, and Vlasta, the continual interaction of the hopeful and more desperate couples in the novel. The characters' names are recorded on the vertical axis while the numbers of the sections in which they appear are listed on the horizontal axis.

TAUBEN IM GRAS

Sections	5	7	13	15	17	18	21	24	25	27	29	31	32	33	36	38	39
Philipp	5	7	13														
Emilia				15	17	18	21										
Washington								24		27	29	31		33			39
Carla									25				32		36	38	
Herr Behrend and Vlasta																38	

Sections (continued)

	40	42	44	45	46	53	54	56	59	60	62	63	64	67	71	73	75	76	77
Philipp	40										62					73			
Emilia												63	64				75		
Washington				45			54	56						67	71			76	77
Carla		42	44			53			59						71				77
Herr Behrend and Vlasta					46					60									

Sections (continued)

	79	82	84	85	88	94	95	96	97	101	102
Philipp		82				94					102
Emilia	79							96	97	101	
Washington				85	88		95				
Carla				85	88		95				
Herr Behrend and Vlasta			84		88						

Notes

Chapter I

[1] Statistical determinism is a term coined by Jean-Paul Sartre in his *Literary and Philosophical Essays*, trans. Annette Michelson (New York: Collier Books, 1962), p. 102. He describes statistical determinism as the modern replacement for the classical concept of fate. In his essay on Dos Passos he explains:

> [Dos Passos' characters], submerged in their own existences, live as they can. They struggle; what comes their way is not determined in advance. And yet, neither their efforts, their faults, nor their most extreme violence can interfere with the regularity of births, marriages and suicides. The pressure exerted by a gas on the walls of its container does not depend upon the individual histories of the molecules composing it.

Unlike his classical ancestors, modern man does not have the luxury of a personally important and determined fate; he is rather ruled by the statistics of modern mass existence.

[2] Eberhard Lämmert, *Bauformen des Erzählens* (Stuttgart: Metzler Verlag, 1967), p. 37.

[3] Franz K. Stanzel, *Typische Formen des Romans* (Gottingen: Vandenhoeck & Ruprecht, 1967), p. 60.

[4] Joseph Warren Beach, *The Twentieth Century Novel: Studies in Techniques* (New York and London: D. Appleton-Century Co., 1932), passim.

[5] In their book *The Nature of Narrative*, Scholes and Kellogg offer an incisive discussion of the shift away from the use of omniscience in narration. See Robert Scholes and Robert Kellogg, *The Nature of Narrative* (New York: Oxford University Press, 1966), pp. 273 ff.

[6] Jerry H. Bryant, in *The Open Decision* (New York: The Free Press, 1970), discusses this same crisis in some detail. He selects slightly different scientific figures on which to focus, and his discussion thus provides a good supplement to my own.

[7] José Ortega y Gasset, *The Modern Theme*, trans. James Cleugh, from the 1923 Spanish version (New York: W.W. Norton and Co., Inc., 1933), p. 79.

[8] Ortega y Gasset, pp. 136-37.

[9] Einstein himself recognized the reflection of his own thoughts and concerns in the works of modern narrative experimenters who substituted multilinearity or intuitive structuring for the more traditional structuring of chronology and causality. See especially his correspondence with Hermann Broch concerning *Der Tod des Vergil* (*The Death of Virgil*) in *Hermann Broch: Gesammelte Werke* (*Briefe von 1929 bis 1951*) (Zürich: Rhein-Verlag, 1957), pp. 227-229.

[10] Henri Bergson, *Time and Free Will*, 1889, trans. Pogson, 1910, pp. 132-34; quoted in A.A. Mendilow, *Time and the Novel* (New York: Humanities Press, 1965), pp. 152-62.

[11] Mendilow comments quite perceptively on the effect of both Freud and Bergson on modern aesthetics in his *Time and the Novel*. See pp. 153 ff.

[12] Sharon Spencer in her book, *Space, Time and Structure in the Modern Novel* (New York: New York University Press, 1971), discusses these issues of reconstituting art and our means of perceiving it. She touches on Döblin's *Berlin Alexanderplatz* and Dos Passos' *USA* in the course of her investigation.

[13] John Hawkes stresses this need to provide a world of meaning within a chaotic universe: "It seems to me necessary to live by creating our own contexts within the constant knowledge of the imminence of annihilation" (an interview quoted by John Kuehl in *John Hawkes and the Craft of Conflict* [New Brunswick, New Jersey: Rutgers University Press, 1975, pp. 160-61]). For other comments by Hawkes on this topic see "A Conversation with John Hawkes" by Paul Emmett and Richard Vine and "The Reader's Voyage through Travesty" by Paul Emmett both in *The Chicago Review* Fall 1976, pp. 163-187.

Chapter II

[1] Descended from a Portuguese grandfather and a Quaker grandmother, John Dos Passos was born in Chicago in 1896. Dos Passos' father, John Randolph Dos Passos, had risen from poverty to the highest levels of the legal profession and the American political scene. John was not publically acknowledged as his father's son until 1916. Married to a mentally ill woman, Dos Passos' father was forced to wait fourteen years until he was free to marry John's mother who was, by that time, nearly an invalid. He and his mother lived apart from his father—much of the time in Europe. His early life in Europe provided settings and specific images that would later appear in *Manhattan Transfer* as Robert Gorham Davis points out:

His years with [his mother] on the Continent gave him vivid memories of places... but he always felt homeless, different from other boys, especially when he went to school in England. His return to America, repeating in a sense his grandfather's immigration, is reflected in the beginning of *Manhattan Transfer*, where Jimmy Herf is seen as a boy debarking from an ocean liner in New York on the Fourth of July.

(From: Robert Gorham Davis, *John Dos Passos* [Minneapolis: University of Minnesota Press, 1962], p. 7.)

Dos Passos entered Harvard in 1912 and wrote literary reviews for the Harvard *Advocate*. In college he would become familiar with Imagist poetry and the works of James Joyce as well as those of Thorstein Veblen. After graduating in 1916, Dos Passos joined the voluntary ambulance service and served in Italy and France. *One Man's Initiation—1917*, a novel based on these wartime experiences, was published in England in 1920 followed by *Three Soldiers* in 1921.

In 1922 Dos Passos' volume of poetry *A Pushcart at the Curb* appeared as well as a collection of essays on Spain, *Rosinante to the Road Again*. This volume reveals Dos Passos' deep attachment to his European heritage and his familiarity with the works of Spanish writers, particularly Pio Baroja's social novels. Dos Passos' play *The Garbage Man* was produced at Harvard in 1925. Presented under the title *The Moon Is a Gong*, the production displayed a debt to the German Expressionist theatre. One more novel, *Streets of Night* (1923), preceded *Manhattan Transfer* (1925). Before returning to New York to write *Manhattan Transfer*, Dos Passos traveled to the East—a trip which provided the material for the travel book *Orient Express* (1927). Another three years elapsed before the appearance of the first volume of the work which was to make Dos Passos a famous as well as controversial writer, the *USA* trilogy (*The 42nd Parallel* [1930], *1919* [1932], and *The Big Money* [1936]).

Dos Passos' shift in political thinking from the left in his younger days to the far right in his later years has greatly complicated his American literary reputation which has continuously vacillated. (George Stade discusses the decline in Dos Passos' reputation after 1939 in his article "The Two Faces of Dos Passos' in *The Partisan Review* 3, Vol. XLI (1974) pp. 476-83. Andrew Hook discusses Dos Passos' overall literary reputation in America in his introduction to *Dos Passos: A Collection of Critical Essays* [Englewood Cliffs, New Jersey: Prentice Hall, 1974].) His effect on European writers, however, has been well documented. (See Ben Stoltzfus' "John Dos Passos and the French" in *Dos Passos, The Critics, and the Writer's Intention*,ed. Belkind [Carbondale: Southern Illinois Univ. Press, 1971] for the effect of Dos Passos' work on the French in particular. Jean-Paul Sartre and Claude-Edmonde Magny also have produced extensive commentary on Dos Passos' work.) The major themes and techniques of *Manhattan Transfer* as well as its overall structural innovations proved fascinating to young Post World War I writers.

[2] George J. Becker, *John Dos Pasos* (New York: Frederick Ungar Publishing Company, 1974), p. 38.

[3] Ibid.

[4]Joseph Warren Beach, *"Manhattan Transfer* Collectivism and Abstract Composition" in *Dos Passos, The Critics, and the Writer's Intention*, ed. Allen Belkind (Carbondale, Ill.: Southern Illinois University Press, 1971), passim.

[5]Beach, pp. 61-62.

[6]John Dos Passos, *Manhattan Transfer* (Boston: Houghton Mifflin Co., Sentry Edition 26, 1925), pp. 235-36. All future page references to the text will be from this edition.

[7]Sinclair Lewis, *John Dos Passos' "Manhattan Transfer"* (New York: Harper and Brothers Publishers, 1926), pp. 20-21.

[8]Whether Jimmy's departure from the city should be read positively or negatively is, apparently, debatable. Joseph Warren Beach sees it as "the protest of the self-determining individual against a world that would make of him a sensual automation" and, therefore, a positive redemptive action (Beach, p. 61). James B. Lane, on the other hand, sees the overall effect of *Manhattan Transfer* as helping to bring down the American success myth in his essay *"Manhattan Transfer* as a Gateway to the 1920's" in *The Centennial Review*, Vol. 16, No. 3 (1972), pp. 293-311. And Blanche H. Gelfant comments that "Twentieth-century Manhattan, as Dos Passos portrays it in an abstract literary picture, embodies the trend away from American ideals of a social system that would allow the individual the fullest opportunity for equality and personal self-fulfillment as a human being" ("John Dos Passos: The Synoptic Novel" in *Dos Passos: A Collection of Critical Essays*, ed. Hook, p. 44).

[9]James B. Lane sees the novel as tending toward naturalism in its themes and details and toward aestheticism in its style in his *"Manhattan Transfer* as a Gateway to the 1920's."

Chapter III

[1]Döblin was in a particularly good position to be familiar both with Berlin as a city and with the underworld characters of the type Franz and Reinhold represent. Döblin spent most of his childhood in Berlin after his father, a tailor, deserted the family to travel to America with a mistress twenty years his junior—an event which was to influence many of Döblin's stories.

Döblin was born in Stettin on August 10, 1878. After the father's desertion, the five Döblin children and their mother moved to Berlin in 1888 where Alfred attended elementary and secondary school. He received his medical degree, with a specialization in psychiatry and neurology, in Freiburgim-Breisgau in 1905. He served part of his internship at the psychiatric hospital Berlin-Buch where Franz Biberkopf was to experience his epiphany. In 1911, Döblin opened a private medical practice in the eastern part of Berlin. Despite the extremely taxing situation and his continuously precarious financial position, Döblin managed to write his first novel *Die drei Sprünge des Wang-lun* (finished in 1913, published in 1915). His first volume of novellas *Die Ermordung einer Butterblume* was published in 1913 and was heavily influenced by his earlier association with German expressionist writers. Döblin spent the war years as a military doctor on the western front and began work on his novel *Wallenstein* (1920).

His work in the poorer sections of Berlin in the inflationary years of the 1920's convinced Döblin of the social responsibility of the writer in a world where technology and social pressures threatened to engulf the individual—a theme treated particularly in his work *Das Ich über der Natur* (1927). Döblin developed a growing and persistent distrust of political parties, however, and in 1921 published a volume of political satires *Der deutsche Maskenball* which called for a socialism free of party bias. The position of the individual within the social collective was to be the theme of Döblin's major works during the 20's—*Berge Meere und Giganten* (1924) and *Manas. Epische Dichtung* (1927).

A trip to Poland in 1924 (recorded in *Reise in Polen* [1925]) revived Döblin's interest in spiritual matters. His experience of the Jewish ghetto of Warsaw convinced him of the astonishing ability of the human spirit to survive under the most difficult circumstances; this realization would prove extremely important in the writing of Franz Biberkopf's story. (Döblin's interest in his Jewish heritage was to continue and increase during his exile in France during World War II.) Another experience during the trip to Poland would provide Döblin with a second major theme of *Berlin Alexanderplatz*. His visit to the Church of St. Mary in Cracow impressed him with the image of the crucified Christ, the man of consciously accepted self-sacrifice whom modern urban man would necessarily learn to emulate.

All of these early experiences were to provide materials for the story of Franz Biberkopf. They lend Döblin's complex depiction of Franz and of Berlin itself a sense of immediacy and reality.

[2] Eds. Ingrid Schuster and Ingrid Bode, *Alfred Döblin im Spiegel der zeitgenössischen Kritik* (Bern: Francke Verlag, 1973), p. 215.

[3] Ibid., p. 218.

[4] Walter Muschg discusses the futurist dynamism of Döblin's style in his Nachwort to the 1971 Deutschen Taschenbuch Verlag edition of *Berlin Alexanderplatz*, p. 416. Wolfgang Kort refers to the narrative techniques as producing "a true image of the chaotic, disconnected, eternally changing—life of the modern city" in *Alfred Döblin* (New York: Twayne Publishers) p. 105. And Wodzimierz Bialik identifies much of Döblin's technique as the reification of chaos in his article "Der Berliner Simplicissimus oder Franz Biberkopf als Exemplum im Spiel der Tranzendenz" in *Bagadnienia Rodzajow Literackich* Tom 29, Zeszyt 1 (36) (1976), pp. 71-72.

[5] Theodore Ziolkowski, *Dimensions of the Modern Novel* (Princeton: Princeton University Press, 1969), p. 123.

[6] Ibid., p. 131.

[7] Ibid., p. 123.

[8] Otto Keller has a particularly interesting interpretation of the biblical figures of Job and Isaac linking them to the Schlachthof scenes in his volume *Brecht und der moderne Roman: Auseinandersetzung Brechts mit den Strukturen der Romane Döblins und Kafkas* (Bern

und München: Francke Verlag, 1975), pp. 7-20.

Keller takes some exception to K. Müller-Salget's reading of the Isaac figure in Müller-Salget's volume *Alfred Döblin, Werk und Entwicklung* (Bonn, 1972).

Andrew M. McLean in "Joyce's *Ulysses* and Döblin's Alexanderplatz Berlin" in *Comparative Literature* Vol. 25, No. 2 (1973), pp. 92-113, also has a short discussion of biblical allusions as parallels to Franz Biberkopf's life.

[9] All page references to the novel are taken from Alfred Döblin, *Berlin Alexanderplatz: Die Geschichte vom Franz Biberkopf* (Olten und Freiburg im Breisgau: Walter, 1967).

[10] Döblin discusses his view of the end of the novel in a letter to Julius Petersen of September 18, 1931. The letter is cited in *Materialien zu Alfred Döblin's Berlin Alexanderplatz*, ed. Matthias Prangel (Frankfurt am Main: Suhrkamp Verlag, 1975), pp. 41-42:

Ein schärferes Urteil über den befremdenden und scheinbar angeklebten Schluß des 'Berlin Alexanderplatz' gewinnt der Verfasser vielleicht noch aus folgender Bemerkung: 1. ist dies Buch als erstes gedacht zu einem zweibändigen. Das zweite sollte (oder soll?) den aktiven Mann, wenn auch nicht dieselbe Person, geben; der Schluß ist sozusagen eine Überbrückung,—aber das andere Ufer fehlt. Dann ist der grundlegende geistige 'Naturalismus' bei mir in eine besondere Conkretionsphase getreten,—es tritt ein mehr passiv-receptives Element mit tragischer Färbung gegen ein aktives Element, das mehr optimistisch ist,—das 'Ich in der Natur' gegen das 'Ich über der Natur.' In 'Berlin Alexanderplatz' wollte ich durchaus den Franz Biberkopf zur zweiten Phase bringen,—es gelang mir nicht. Gegen meinen Willen, einfach aus der Logik der Handlung und des Plans endete das Buch so; es war rettungslos, mir schwammen meine Felle davon. Der Schluß müßte—eigentlich im Himmel spielen, schon wieder eine Seele gerettet, na, das war nicht möglich, aber ich ließ es mir nicht nehmen, zum Schluß Fanfaren zu blasen, es mochte psychologisch stimmen oder nicht. Bisher sehe ich: der Dualismus ist nicht aufzuheben. —Ich empfehle besonders dem Verfasser zur Vertiefung noch mein vorletztes Buch 'Manas,' dies Versepos, su lesen; der Biberkopf ist da vorgebildet,—und die Kluft ist auf indisch-mystische Weise, eine Wiedergeburt, überbrückt.

The author will perhaps form a sharper judgment of the disconcerting and apparently tacked-on ending of *Berlin Alexanderplatz* from the following remarks: First, this book was originally intended to be the first of two volumes. The second was supposed to (or is supposed to?) present the active man, even if not the same person [Biberkopf]; the ending is, so to speak, a transition, a bridge—but the other bank is missing. Second, the basic, intellectual "Naturalism" in my work reached a particular phase of solidification for me,—a more passive-receptive element with tragic overtones confronted the active element, which is more optimistic, —the "self in nature" confronted "the self above nature." In *Berlin Alexanderplatz* I definitely wanted to bring Franz Biberkopf to the second phase, —I didn't succeed. Against my will, simply out of the logic of the action and the plot my book ended as it did; it was unsalvageable. The ending really had to be played in heaven—one more soul saved, well, that wasn't possible, but I couldn't pass up the opportunity to blow the fanfare at the end, whether it was psychologically plausible or not. Now I see that the duality cannot be abolished. —I recommend particularly that the author read, for deeper understanding, my next to last book *Manas*, the verse epic; Biberkopf is prefigured there, —and the chasm is bridged in Indian-mystical manner, a rebirth.

[11] Leon L. Titche, Jr. discusses the use of the Orestes motif in "Döblin and Dos Passos: Aspects of the City Novel" in *Modern Fiction Studies*, Vol. 17, No. 1 (1971), pp. 125-35. Further discussion can be found in Dieter Baacke's "Erzähltes Engagement—Antike Mythologie in Döblins Romanen," *Text und Kritik* 13/14 (1966).

Chapter IV

[1] Descended from an old Mississippi family, Faulkner had ready access to the rural milieu of the Bundren Family. Born September 25, 1897 in New Albany, Mississippi, Faulkner was the oldest son of Murry and Maud Falkner and the great-grandson of Col. William Cuthbert Falkner, the prototype of Col. Sartoris in *Sartoris* and *The Unvanquished*. In 1902 the family moved to Oxford, Mississippi where Faulkner's father would eventually become business manager of the University of Mississippi.

In 1918 Faulkner trained in the Canadian Air Force but never saw active duty in World War I. His flight training would later prove useful, however, as he flew with a barnstormers group in 1925. He briefly attended the University of Mississippi and would eventually serve as its postmaster for a short period in 1921. In 1920 Faulkner experienced the modern urban setting of New York City where he clerked in the Doubleday Bookshop at Lord and Taylors. The shop was managed by Elizabeth Prall, the future bride of Sherwood Anderson who would sponsor Faulkner's novel *Soldier's Pay* (1925) and would be one of the central figures in Faulkner's *Sherwood Anderson and Other Famous Creoles* (1926).

In 1924 Faulkner published a book of verse, *The Marble Faun*. During 1925 he lived in New Orleans and associated with the "Double Dealer" group which included Roark Bradford, Lyle Saxon, Oliver La Farge and Sherwood Anderson. Faulkner made a brief trip to Europe with William Spratling and spent some time in Paris.

In 1929 in the novel *Sartoris*, Faulkner created his fictional Yoknapatawpha County through which the Bundren family would eventually make its burial journey. *The Sound and the Fury* appeared in the same year, during which Faulkner also married and settled in Oxford. While working the night shift at the power plant of the University, Faulkner wrote *As I Lay Dying* which appeared in 1930. The following year marked the appearance of *Sanctuary*, the novel that was to make Faulkner a popular success. In 1950 Faulkner was awarded the Nobel prize for literature. During his acceptance speech, Faulkner expressed a theme central to many of his major novels including *As I Lay Dying*: "that man will not merely endure: he will prevail...because he has a soul, a spirit capable of compassion and sacrifice and endurance."

[2] All page references to the novel are taken from William Faulkner, *As I Lay Dying* (New York: Vintage Books, 1964).

[3] A number of critics have investigated individual characters from the novel, frequently engaging in what might be called the "name game"—an attempt to link characters allusively to classical, Old and New Testament counterparts. Is Cora, for example, related to the Greek Kore, as Carvel Collins suggests? (Carvel Collins, "The Pairing of *The Sound and the Fury* and *As I Lay Dying*," *Princeton University Library Chronicle*, 18 [1957], 114-23.) Or is she rather representative of the Old Testament Korah, as Joseph Gold posits? (Joseph Gold, "Sin, Salvation and Bananas: *As I Lay Dying*," *Mosaic*, No. 17 [1973], 63-73.) Or, in less homonymic parallels, is Cash Hephaestos, as Elizabeth Kerr states (Elizabeth M. Kerr, "*As I Lay Dying* as Ironic Quest," *Wisconsin Studies in Contemporary Literature*, 3 [Winter 1962], 5-19), or rather a Christ figure, as Robert Reed Sanderlin points out? (Robert Reed Sanderlin, "*As I Lay Dying*: Christian Symbols and Thematic Implications," *The Southern Quarterly*, Vol. 7, No. 2 [1969], 155-66.) Is Whitfield related to Hawthorne's Dimmesdale (Richard Bridgman, "As Hester Prynne Lay Dying," *English Language Notes*, 2 [June 1965], 294-96) or to Rev. George Whitefield? (Gold.) The allegorical readings are frequently quite creative and persuasive; they point to the allusive richness of the text. But one is left with the feeling that they do not quite cohere satisfactorily, that they do not, finally, elucidate the novel as a whole.

[4] Claude Lévi-Strauss, "The Structural Study of Myth" *Structural Anthropology*, trans. Claire Jakobson and Brooke Schoept (New York: Basic Books, Inc., 1963), p. 214.

[5] Some critics have sought to unravel the novel's structure by other approaches. Joseph W. Reed has done an extensive analysis of the narrative rhythm of *As I Lay Dying* based upon types of transitions between various narrators and on the modulation of kin and non-kin speakers. (Joseph W. Reed, Jr., *Faulkner's Narrative* [New Haven: Yale University Press, 1973].) Andre Bleikasten offers a somewhat metaphorical interpretation of the novel's structure in terms of a linear pattern produced by the burial journey and a second, circular pattern created by the use of Addie Bundren as the central focus of the novel. His linear and circular patterns escalate to an image of the spiral as he attempts to clarify his impressions of the novel's dynamic structure, but his discussion remains essentially metaphorical. (Andre Bleikasten, *Faulkner's "As I Lay Dying"* [Bloomington: Indiana University Press, 1973], p. 49.)

[6] M.E. Bradford argues that Addie, the " 'I' who is still dying until the narrative concludes, is the auditor of all the reveries" (M.E. Bradford, "Addie Bundren and the Design of *As I Lay Dying*," *The Southern Review*, Vol. 6, No. 4 [Autumn 1970], 1094) which make up the text. Addie's ghost-like presence is thus responsible for the selection, weight, and arrangement of the narrative sections. David Monaghan, on the other hand, proposes that Addie is the single narrator of the novel which becomes a record of her stream-of-consciousness. (David M. Monaghan, "The Single Narrator of *As I Lay Dying*," *Modern Fiction Studies*, 18 [Summer 1972], 213-20.) Paul Lilly takes a somewhat different tack in seeing Addie's centrality as dependent upon the extent to which her use of language approximates Faulkner's idea of the impeccable, absolute perfection of poetry. (Paul R. Lilly, Jr., "Caddie and Addie: Speakers of Faulkner's Impeccable Language," *The Journal of Narrative Technique*, Vol. 3, No. 3, 170-82.) And in *Faulkner's Women* Sally R. Page adds a

sensitive character analysis to the critical material on Addie as a central character. (Sally R. Page, *Faulkner's Women: Characterization and Meaning* [Florida: Everett/Edwards Inc., 1972], 111-35.)

[7] I do not feel, as Reed implies, that we so totally identify with Darl's vision. We do, indeed, feel a closeness to him and sympathy for his poetic sensitivity; but were we to let "his view become our norm, his prophecy, his poetry, his abstraction become our habit of thinking" (p. 89), we would be at a loss to deal with the reunification of the Bundren family at Darl's expense.

[8] Robert M. Slabey's *"As I Lay Dying* as an Existential Novel" (*Bucknell Review*, 11 [Dec. 1963], 12-23) and Robert Hemenway's "Enigmas of Being in *As I Lay Dying*" (*Modern Fiction Studies*, 16 [Summer 1970], 133-46) see the novel as presenting a range of possible strategies for dealing with existence, of possible modes of living as represented in the attitudes of various characters.

[9] Slabey, p. 22.

[10] Vardaman is not, I think, "temporarily insane" as Slabey argues (p. 17), but rather has an unconscious capacity to create myth to deal with reality as Enrico Garzilli implies in *Circles Without Center* (Cambridge: Harvard Univ. Press, 1972), pp. 61-62. Robert L. Nadeau presents a perceptive analysis of the actual process of Vardaman's transference of meaning in the identification of Addie and the fish in "The Morality of Act: A Study of Faulkner's *As I Lay Dying*," *Mosaic*, Vol. 6, No. 3 (1973), 23-35.

[11] Malcolm Cowley, ed., *Writers at Work* (New York: Viking Press, 1958), p. 129.

[12] Robert Penn Warren in "Introduction: Faulkner: Past and Future," *Faulkner: A Collection of Critical Essays* (Englewood Cliffs, N.J.: Prentice-Hall, Inc., 1966) cites the struggle of the individual consciousness with the larger patterns of life:

> [Faulkner's work] springs from...a need...to struggle with the painful incoherences and paradoxes of life, and with the contradictory and often unworthy impulses and feelings in the self, in order to achieve meaning; but to struggle, in the awareness that meaning, if achieved, will always rest in perilous balance, and that the great undergirding and overarching meaning of life is in the act of trying to create meaning through struggle (pp. 14-15).

In the same collection of essays, George Marion O'Donnell notes the conflict of the individual identity with archetypal, mythic significance in his essay "Faulkner's Mythology."

> The Sartorises and the Sutpens and the Compsons...are people, in a certain way of life, at a particular time, confronted with real circumstances and with items of history. And their humanity (or their illusion of humanity, on a larger-than-life scale) is not limited, ultimately, by their archetypal significance. Moreover, in each book there is a dramatically credible fiction which remains particular and (sometimes with difficulty) coherent as action, even though the pattern is true, in a larger sense, as myth (pp. 27-28).

Furthermore, Faulkner's preoccupation with the structural possibilities of narrative hardly needs to be argued. As Conrad Aiken points out in "William Faulkner: The Novel As Form," *Faulkner: A Collection of Critical Essays*:

> What immoderately delights him, alike in *Sanctuary, The Sound and the Fury, As I Lay Dying, Light in August, Pylon, Absalom, Absalom!*, and now again in *The Wild Palms*, and what sets him above—shall we say it firmly—all his American contemporaries, is his continuous preoccupation with the novel *as form*, his passionate concern with it, and a degree of success with it which would clearly have commanded the interest and respect of Henry James himself (p. 49).

[13] Slabey, pp. 17-18.

[14] Slabey, p. 18.

[15] Slabey, p. 17.

Chapter V

[1] We could equally well follow other specific lines of development. The structural innovations of Döblin could, for example, be traced to the works of Günther Grass who acknowledges his debt to Döblin's work. Or we could follow the multilinear variations of Faulkner's novels to their successors in the works of Heinrich Böll. Koeppen's *Tauben im Gras*, however, will provide a particularly propitious object of investigation for reasons which will become evident as we proceed.

Wolfgang Koeppen's literary career is rather unusual in that he has not published a major work since the last volume of his travel journals over twenty years ago. This silence on Koeppen's part has become the center of endless speculations as to whether the cause is political as Marcel Reich-Ranicki maintains (in "Der Fall Wolfgang Koeppen" in *Über Wolfgang Koeppen*, ed. Ulrich Greiner [Suhrkamp Verlag: Frankfurt am Main, 1976), pp. 101-08), or aesthetic as Rehnhard Döhl (in "Wolfgang Koeppen" in *Deutsche Literatur seit 1945 in Einzeldarstellungen*, ed. Dietrich Weber [Stuttgart: A. Kröner, 1968], 103-29) and Helmut Heissenbüttel (in "Wolfgang Koeppen—Kommentar" in *Merkur* 22 [1968], 244-52) suggest, or personal as Christian Linder hints (in "Schreiben als Zustand: Ein Gespräch mit Wolfgang Koeppen" in *Text + Kritik*, ed. Heinz Ludwig Arnold [München: Edition Text und Kritik, April 1972, Heft 34] *Wolfgang Koeppen*, pp. 14-32). Alfred Andersch in his essay "Die Geheimschreiber" (*Merkur* 30, Heft 6 (1976), pp. 555-63) argues that the entire problem of Koeppen's "writing block" is spurious, that it is not a question of Koeppen's not writing but of his not publishing. Andersch attributes this reluctance to Koeppen's ongoing search for a literary form compatible with the changed political and cultural situation of the 60's and 70's. Josef Quack (in "Die Haltung des Beobachters: Pauschale Überlegungen auf Wolfgang Koeppen" in *Frankfurter Hefte: Zeitschrift zur Kultur und Politik*, 29. Heft 11 (1974), pp. 823-34) indicates a similar but more radical cultural disjunction between the present mass-culture and Koeppen's earlier aesthetic forms, arguing that the ideal of individual self-fulfillment on which the bourgeois novel form had been based has no place in a modern, technological culture. Koeppen, according to Quack, has therefore reached the end of the novel's literary possibilities. At any rate, Koeppen's silence has nearly merited more critical comment than his actual literary productions. To aggravate the situation, Koeppen has shown a marked evasiveness when asked for either his explanation of his silence or a more detailed description of his personal biography.

Koeppen was born June 23, 1906 in Greifswald. He spent a good deal of his childhood with an uncle who was a mathematician and who tacitly allowed him to avoid much of his early formal schooling. Koeppen held a number of different jobs including those of ship's cook and eventually journalist. Like Dos Passos, Koeppen was a voracious reader and traveled almost constantly. Koeppen also resembled both Dos Passos and Döblin in his keen political awareness coupled with a distrust of formal political parties.

Koeppen's first novel *Eine unglückliche Liebe* appeared in 1934 followed by *Die Mauer Schwankt* in 1935. During the war years Koeppen fled to Holland and did not publish again until 1951 when *Tauben im Gras* appeared followed by *Das Treibhaus* in 1953 and *Der Tod im Rom* in 1954. After the writing of his post-war trilogy, Koeppen turned his attention to travel literature and essays, publishing *Nach Russland und anderswohin* (1958), *Amerika-Fahrt* (1959), and *Reisen nach Frankreich* (1961). Since that time he has written only short newspaper and magazine articles. He received the Georg-Büchner-Preis in 1962.

[2] Many critics of Koeppen's work have cited its relationship to earlier multilinear novels. Georg Bungter in "Über Wolfgang Koeppens *Tauben im Gras*" (in *Zeitschrift für Deutsche Philologie,*Band 87, Heft 4 [1968], pp. 535-45) links Koeppen to Faulkner, Dos Passos, and Joyce. Stanley Craven in "Two Novels by Wolfgang Koeppen" (*Modern Languages*, Vol. 51, No. 4 [1970], pp. 167-72) adds Virginia Woolf to the list of Koeppen's literary forebears. Finally, Manfred Koch (*Wolfgang Koeppen: Literatur zwischen Nonkonformismus und Resignation*, [Stuttgart: Verlag W. Kohlhammer, 1973]), Wolfdietrich Rasch ("Wolfgang Koeppen" in *Deutsche Dichter der Gegenwart*, ed. Benno von Wiese [Berlin: Erich Schmidt Verlag, 1973], pp. 210-30), and Marcel Reich-Ranicki ("Der Zeuge Koeppen" in *Über Wolfgang Koeppen*, ed. Ulrich Greiner [Frankfurt am Main: Suhrkamp Verlag, 1976], pp.133-50) all tie Koeppen's stylistic innovations directly to Dos Passos' *Manhattan Transfer* and Döblin's *Berlin Alexanderplatz*.

[3] Horst Bienek, "Gespräch mit Wolfgang Koeppen" in *H.B.: Werkstattgespräche mit Schriftstellern* (München: C. Hanser, 1965), p. 59.

[4] Manfred Koch, *Wolfgang Koeppen: Literatur zwischen Nonkonformismus und Resignation* (Stuttgart: Verlag W. Kohlhammer, 1973), p. 65.

[5] Stanley Craven, "Two Novels by Wolfgang Koeppen," passim.

[6] There is some uncertainty as to this number. Most sections are separated by a physical space in the printed page. If one takes only those sections thus set off in print, the total number of discrete passages would equal 98. There are five additional passages in which both the characters and the physical setting shift, but without the corresponding spacing to make a new section. In all other such circumstances, Koeppen creates a discrete passage, a fact which implies perhaps that the printer overlooked some spacing. If so, the number of

passages would equal 103. Manfred Koch suggests that there are 106 individual passages (*Wolfgang Koeppen*, p. 64). There are two scenes in which the characters change but the setting, a stadium featuring the Red Star's baseball game, remains unchanged. If Koch also separated these passages he would have arrived at the higher number he cites. This analysis and all future page references to the novel are from Wolfgang Koeppen, *Tauben im Gras, Das Treibhaus, Der Tod im Rom* (Einbändige Sonderausgabe der Romane), (Stuttgart: Henry Goverts Verlag, 1969).

[7] Manfred Koch sees the shift to present tense in the closing passages as an "Appell des Autors an sein Publikum, in der realen geschichtlichen Lebenspraxis nicht hinter die im Roman antizipierten beängstigenden Erfahrungen zurückzufallen, sondern Gesellschafts-modelle zu entwickeln, die eine humanere Existenz als die der Romangestalten ermöglichen" (Koch, p. 75). ("an appeal by the author to his public not to fall back into the alarming experiences anticipated in the novel in the real, historical affairs of life, but to develop models of society which make possible a more humane existence than that of the characters in the novel.)

[8] See Volker Klotz, *Die Erzählte Stadt* (München: C. Hanser, 1969).

[9] Klaus Haberkamm, "Wolfgang Koeppen: 'Bienenstock des Teufels'—zum naturhaft-mythischen Geschichts—und Gesellschaftsbild in den Nachkriegsromanen" in *Zeitkritische Romane des 20. Jahrhunderts*, ed. Hans Wagener (Stuttgart: Philipp Reclam Verlag, 1975), p. 264.

[10] Letter from Koeppen to Cecile Cazort-Zorach dated 17 Juli 1975.

Chapter VI

[1] Jean-Paul Sartre, *Literary and Philosophical Essays*, trans. Annette Michelson (New York: Collier Books, 1962), p. 102.

[2] Sartre, p. 102.

Bibliography

General Theory

Allott, Miriam. *Novelists on the Novel*. New York: Columbia University Press, 1959.

Barthes, Roland. *Sur Racine*. Paris: Editions de Seuil, 1963.

Beach, Joseph Warren. *American Fiction 1920-1940*. New York: The Macmillan Company, 1948.

_____. *The Twentieth Century Novel: Studies in Techniques*. New York and and London: D. Appleton-Century Company, 1932.

Booth, Wayne C. *The Rhetoric of Fiction*. Chicago: University of Chicago Press, 1961.

Bryant, Jerry H. *The Open Decision*. New York: The Free Press, 1970.

Culler, Jonathan. *Structuralist Poetics*. Ithaca: Cornell University Press, 1975.

Emmet, Paul and Vine, Richard. "A Conversation with John Hawkes." *The Chicago Review* (Fall 1976), pp. 163-171.

Emmet, Paul. "The Reader's Voyage through Travesty." *The Chicago Review* (Fall 1976), pp. 172-183.

Frank, Joseph. *The Widening Gyre*. Bloomington: Indiana University Press, 1963.

Freedman, Ralph. *The Lyrical Novel*. Princeton: Princeton University Press, 1963.

Greimas, A.J. *Semantique Structurale*. Paris: Larousse, 1966.

Gullon, Ricardo. "On Space in the Novel." *Critical Inquiry*, Vol. 2, No. 1 (1975), pp. 11-28.

Günther, Hans. *Struktur als Prozess*. München: Wilhelm Fink Verlag, 1973.

Hamburger, Käte. *The Logic of Literature*. Trans. Marilynn Rose. Bloomington: Indiana University Press, 1973.

Hauser, Arnold. *The Social History of Art*. Vol. 4. Trans. Stanley Godman. New York: Vintage Books, 1951.

Heller, Erich. *The Disinherited Mind*. New York: Meridian Books, 1959.

James, Henry. *The Art of the Novel*. New York: Charles Scribner's Sons, 1907.

Jakobson, Roman. *Essais de linguistique generale*. Paris: Editions de Minuit, 1963.

Krutch, Joseph Wood. *The Modern Temper: A Study and a Confession*. New York: Harcourt, 1933.

Kuehl, John. *John Hawkes and the Craft of Conflict*. New Brunswick, New Jersey: Rutgers University Press, 1975.

Lämmert, Eberhard. *Bauformen des Erzählens*. Stuttgart: J.B. Metzler Verlag, 1955.

Lane, Michael, ed. *Introduction to Structuralism*. New York: Basic Books, 1970.

Lévi-Strauss, Claude. *Structural Anthropology*. Trans. Claire Jacobson and Brooke Grundfest Schoepf. New York: Basic Books, 1963.

Lukács, Georg. *The Theory of the Novel*. Trans. Anna Bostock. Cambridge, Mass: MIT Press, 1971.

Magny, Claude-Edmonde. *The Age of the American Novel: The Film Aesthetic of Fiction Between the Two Wars*. Trans. Eleanor Hochman. New York: Frederick Ungar Publishing Company, 1972.

Mendilow, A.A. *Time and the Novel*. New York: Humanities Press, 1952, rpt. 1965.

Müller, Günther. *Morphologische Poetik*. Tübingen: Max Niemeyer Verlag, 1968.

O'Connor, William Van, ed. *Forms of Modern Fiction*. Bloomington: Indiana University Press, 1963.

Ortega y Gasset, José. *The Dehumanizations of Art and Other Essays on Art, Culture, and Literature*. Trans. Helene Weyl from the 1925 Spanish edition. Princeton: Princeton University Press, 1969.

_____. *The Modern Theme*. Trans. James Cleugh from the 1923 Spanish edition. New York: W.W. Norton & Co., Inc., 1933.

Piaget, Jean. *Structuralism*. Trans. Chaninah Maschler. New York: Harper Torchbooks, 1971.

Rosenthal, Erwin Theodor. *Das fragmentarische Universum: Wege und Umwege des modernen Romans*. München: Nymphenburger Verlagshandlung, 1970.

Sartre, Jean-Paul. *Literary and Philosophical Essays*. Trans. Annette Michelson. New York: Collier Books, 1955.

Scholes, Robert, ed. *Approaches to the Novel: Materials for a Poetics*. Scranton: Chandler Publishing Co., 1961.

Scholes, Robert and Robert Kellogg. *The Nature of Narrative*. New York: Oxford University Press, 1966.

Sokel, Walter. *The Writer in Extremis*. Stanford: Stanford University Press, 1959.

Spencer, Sharon. *Space, Time and Structure in The Modern Novel*. New York: New York University Press, 1971.

Stanzel, Franz. *Narrative Situations in the Novel*. Trans. James Pusack. Bloomington: Indiana University Press, 1971.

_____. *Typische Formen des Romans*. Göttingen: Vandenhoeck & Ruprecht, 1967.

Stevick, Philip, ed. *The Theory of the Novel*. New York: The Free Press (Macmillan Publishing, Inc.), 1967.

Todorov, Tzvetan. *Poetique de la Prose*. Paris: Editions du Seuil, 1965.

_____. "Structural Analysis of Narrative" *Novel*, Vol. 3, No. 1 (1969), pp. 70-76.

_____, ed. *Theorie de la Litterature*. Paris: Editions du Seuil, 1965.

Watt, Ian. *The Rise of the Novel*. Berkeley: The University of California Press, 1971.

Ziolkowski, Theodore. *Dimensions of the Modern Novel: German Texts and European Contexts*. Princeton: Princeton University Press, 1969.

John Dos Passos

Astre, Georges-Albert. *Themes et Structures dans l'oeuvre de John Dos Passos*. Paris: Lettres Modernes, 1956.

Beach, Joseph Warren. "*Manhattan Transfer*: Collectivism and Abstract Composition." In *Dos Passos, The Critics, and the Writer's Intention*. Ed. Allen Belkind. Carbondale: Southern Illinois University Press, 1971, pp. 54-69.

Becker, George J. *John Dos Passos*. New York: Frederick Ungar Publishing Co., 1974.

Belkind, Allen, ed. *Dos Passos, The Critics, and the Writer's Intention*. Carbondale: Southern Illinois University Press, 1971.

Cowley, Malcolm. "Dos Passos and His Critics." *New Republic*, 120 (1949), pp. 21-23.

Davis, Robert Gorham. *John Dos Passos*. Minneapolis: University of Minnesota Press, 1962.

Diggins, John P. "Visions of Chaos and Visions of Order: Dos Passos as Historian?" *American Literature*, Vol. 46, No. 3 (1974), pp. 329-46.

Dos Passos, John. *Manhattan Transfer*. Boston: Houghton Mifflin Company, 1925.

Geismar, Maxwell. "John Dos Passos: Conversion of a Hero." In *Writers in Crisis*. Boston: Houghton Mifflin Company, 1942, pp. 87-139.

Gelfant, Blanche H. "John Dos Passos: The Synoptic Novel." In *Dos Passos: A Collection of Critical Essays*. Englewood Cliffs, New Jersey: Prentice-Hall, Inc., 1974, pp. 36-52.

Hook, Andrew, ed. *Dos Passos: A Collection of Critical Essays*. Englewood Cliffs, New Jersey: Prentice-Hall, Inc., 1974.

Krysinski, Wladimin. "Le 'Paralittéraire' et le 'Littéraire' dans le Texte Romanesque Moderne." *Zagadnienia Rodzajow Literackich*, Tom 29, Zeszyt 1(36) (1976), pp. 53-67.

Lane, James B. "*Manhattan Transfer* as a Gateway to the 1920's." *The Centennial Review*, Vol. 16, No. 3 (1972), pp. 239-311.

Lewis, Sinclair. *John Dos Passos' "Manhattan Transfer."* New York: Harper and Brothers Publishers, 1926.

Lowry, E.D. "Dos Passos' *Manhattan Transfer* und die Technik des Films" In *Der Amerikanische Roman im 19. und 20. Jahrhundert*. Berlin: Erich Schmidt Verlag, 1974, pp. 238-257.

Magee, John David. "An Analytic Study of John Dos Passos' *Manhattan Transfer*." Diss. Ball State University, 1971.

Neuse, Werner, *Die literarische Entwicklung von John Dos Passos*. Giessen: Buchdruckerei Richard Glagow, 1931.

Stade, George. "The Two Faces of Dos Passos." *The Partisan Review*, Vol. 41 (1974), pp. 476-83.

Stoltzfus, Ben. "John Dos Passos and the French." In *Dos Passos, The Critics and the Writer's Intention*. Carbondale: Southern Illinois University Press, 1971, pp. 197-218.

Alfred Döblin

Beyer, Manfred. "Die Entstehungsgeschichte von Alfred Döblins Roman *Berlin Alexanderplatz*." *Wissenschaftliche Zeitschrift der Friedrich-Schiller Universität Jena*, 20. Jahrgang, Heft 3 (1971), pp. 391-423.

Bialik, Wlodzimierz. "Der Berliner Simplicissimus oder Franz Biberkopf als Exemplum im Spiel der Tranzendenz." *Zagadnienia Rodzajow Literackich*, Tom 29, Zeszyt 1(36) (1976), pp. 69-84.

Bode, Ingrid and Ingrid Schuster, eds. *Alfred Döblin im Spiegel der zeitgenössischen Kritik*. Bern: Francke Verlag, 1973.

Döblin, Alfred, "Der Bau des Epischen Werks." In *Aufsätze zur Literatur*. Ed. Walter Muschg. Olten und Freiburg im Breisgau: Walter, 1963, pp. 103-132.

_____. *Berlin Alexanderplatz: Die Geschichte vom Franz Biberkopf.* Olten und Freiburg im Breisgau: Walter, 1967.

_____. *Doktor Döblin: Selbstbiographie von Alfred Döblin.* Berlin: Friedenauer Press, 1970.

Duytschaever, Joris. "Joyce-Dos Passos-Döblin: Einfluss oder Analogie?" In *Materialien zu Alfred Döblin's "Berlin Alexanderplatz."* Ed. Matthias Prangel. Frankfurt: Suhrkamp, 1975, pp. 136-49.

Hitzer, Hartmut. "Einige Überlegungen zum gegenwärtigen Stand der Döblin-Bibliographie am Beispiel von Louis Hugets *Bibliographie Alfred Döblin.*" *Euphorion,* 69. Band, 1. Heft (1975), pp. 86-99.

Keller, Otto. *Brecht und der moderne Roman.* Bern: Francke Verlag, 1975.

Klotz, Volker. *Die Erzählte Stadt.* München: C. Hanser, 1969.

Kort, Wolfgang. *Alfred Döblin.* New York: Twayne Publishers, Inc., 1974.

Kreutzer, Leo. *Alfred Döblin: Sein Werk bis 1933.* Stuttgart: Kohlhammer, 1970.

Lewis, Kathleen Buford. "The Representation of Social Space in the Novel: *Manhattan Transfer, Naked Year,* and *Berlin Alexanderplatz.*" Diss. University of Iowa, 1976.

McCoy, Ingeborg Hedwig Rüberg. "Realism and Surrealism in the Works of Alfred Döblin: The Aspect of the Demonic". Diss. University of Texas, Austin, 1972.

McLean, Andrew M. "Joyce's *Ulysses* and Döblin's *Alexanderplace Berlin.*" *Comparative Literature,* Vol. 25, No. 2. (1972), pp. 92-113.

Minder, Robert. "Alfred Döblin." In *Deutsche Literatur im zwanzigsten Jahrhundert.* Ed. Hermann Friedmann and Otto Mann. 2nd edition; Heidelberg: Wolfgang Rothe, 1956, pp. 140-160.

Mitchell, Breon. *James Joyce and The German Novel 1922-1933.* Athens, Ohio: Ohio University Press, 1976.

_____. "Joyce and Döblin: At the Crossroads of *Berlin Alexanderplatz.*" *Contemporary Literature,* Vol. 12, No. 2 (1971), pp. 173-187.

Prangel, Matthias. *Alfred Döblin.* Stuttgart: J.B. Metzlersche Verlagsbuchhandlung, 1973.

_____. ed. *Materialien zu Alfred Döblins "Berlin Alexanderplatz."* Frankfurt: Suhrkamp Verlag, 1975.

Schöne, Albrecht. "Döblin: *Berlin Alexanderplatz.*" In *Der deutsche Roman vom Barock bis zur Gegenwart.* Ed. Benno von Wiese. Düsseldorf: Bagel, 1963, pp. 291-325.

Schoonover, Henrietta. "The Humorous and Grotesque Elements in Döblin's *Berlin Alexanderplatz.*" Diss. McGill University, 1974.

Schwimmer, Helmut. *Alfred Döblin: Berlin Alexanderplatz.* Munich: R. Oldenbourg Verlag, 1973.

Titche, Leon L. "Döblin and Dos Passos: Aspects of the City Novel." *Modern Fiction Studies*, Vol. 17, No. 1 (1971), pp. 125-135.

Ziolkowski, Theodore. *Dimensions of the Modern Novel: German Texts and European Contexts*. Princeton: Princeton University Press, 1969.

William Faulkner

Alexandrescu, Sorin, "Logic du Personnage: reflexions sur l'univers Faulknerien." In *Univers Semiotiques*. Ed. A.J. Greimas. France: Maison Mame, 1974.

Bleikasten, Andre. *Faulkner's "As I Lay Dying."* Trans. Roger Little. Bloomington: Indiana University Press, 1973.

Bradford, M.E. "Addie Bundren and the Design of *As I Lay Dying*." *The Southern Review*, Vol. 6, No. 4 (1970), pp. 1039-99.

Bridgman, Richard. "As Hester Prynne Lay Dying." *English Language Notes*, 2 (1965), pp. 294-96.

Collins, Carvel. "The Pairing of *The Sound and the Fury* and *As I Lay Dying*." *Princeton University Library Chronicle*, 18 (1957), pp. 114-23.

Cowley, Malcolm, ed. *Writers at Work: The Paris Review Interviews*. New York: Viking Press, 1958.

Faulkner, William. *As I Lay Dying*. New York: Vintage Books, 1964.

Garzilli, Enrico. *Circles Without Center*. Cambridge: Harvard Univ. Press, 1972.

Gold, Joseph. "Sin, Salvation and Bananas: *As I Lay Dying*." *Mosaic*, No. 17 (1973), pp. 63-73.

Gwynn, Frederick L., and Joseph L. Blotner, eds. *Faulkner in the University*. Charlottesville, Virginia: Univ. of Virginia Press, 1959.

Hemenway, Robert. "Enigmas of Being in *As I Lay Dying*." *Modern Fiction Studies*, 16 (1970), pp. 133-146.

Iser, Wolfgang. *Der Implizite Leser*. Munich: Wilhelm Fink Verlag, 1972.

Kerr, Elizabeth M. *"As I Lay Dying* as Ironic Quest." *Wisconsin Studies in Contemporary Literature*, 3 (1962), pp. 5-19.

——————. *Yoknapatawpha: Faulkner's "Little Postage Stamp of Native Soil."* New York: Fordham University Press, 1969.

Lilly, Paul R. "Caddie and Addie: Speakers of Faulkner's Impeccable Language." *The Journal of Narrative Technique*, Vol. 3, No. 3 (1973), pp. 170-182.

Meriwether, James, and Michael Millgate, eds. *Lion in the Garden: Interviews with William Faulkner (1926-62)*. New York: Random House, 1968.

Millgate, Michael. *William Faulkner: A Collection of Criticism.* New York: McGraw-Hill, 1973.

Monaghan, David M. "The Single Narrator of *As I Lay Dying.*" *Modern Fiction Studies,* 18 (1972), pp. 213-20.

Nadeau, Robert L. "The Morality of Act: A Study of Faulkner's *As I Lay Dying.*" *Mosaic,* Vol. 6, No. 3 (1973), pp. 23-35.

Page, Sally R. *Faulkner's Women: Characterization and Meaning.* Florida: Everett/ Edwards, Inc., 1972.

Reed, Joseph W. *Faulkner's Narrative.* New Haven: Yale University Press, 1973.

Richardson, H. Edward. *William Faulkner: The Journey to Self-Discovery.* Columbia: University of Missouri Press, 1969.

Sanderlin, Robert Reed. *"As I Lay Dying*: Christian Symbols and Thematic Implications." *The Southern Quarterly,* Vol. 7, No. 2 (1969), pp. 155-66.

Schmitter, Dean Morgan, ed. *William Faulkner: A Collection of Criticism.* New York: McGraw-Hill, 1973.

Slabey, Robert M. "*As I Lay Dying* as an Existential Novel." *Bucknell Review,* 11 (1963), pp. 12-23.

Ulrich, Michaela. *Perspektive und Erzählstruktur in William Faulkners Romanen.* Heidelberg: Carl Winter Universitätsverlag, 1972.

Vickery, Olga W. *The Novels of William Faulkner.* Louisiana: Louisiana State University Press, 1959.

Warren, Robert Penn, ed. *Faulkner: A Collection of Critical Essays.* Englewood Cliffs, New Jersey: Prentice-Hall, Inc., 1966.

Wolfgang Koeppen

Andersch, Alfred. "Die Geheimschreiber." *Merkur,* 30. Jahrgang, Heft 6 (1976) pp. 555-63.

Arnold, Heinz Ludwig. *Gespräche mit Schriftstellen.* München: Verlag C.H. Beck, 1975.

_____. ed. *Text + Kritik.* Heft 34 *Wolfgang Koeppen.* München: Edition Text und Kritik, 1972.

Bienek, Horst. "Gespräch mit Wolfgang Koeppen." in *H.B.: Werkstattgespräche mit Schriftstellern.* München: C. Hanser, 1964.

Bungter, Georg. "Über Wolfgang Koeppens *Tauben im Gras.*" *Zeitschrift für Deutsche Philologie,* Band 87, Heft 4 (1968), pp. 535-45.

Craven, Stanley. "Two Novels by Wolfgang Koeppen—*Tauben im Gras* and *Das Treibhaus.*" *Modern Languages*, Vol. 11, No. 4 (1970), pp. 167-72.

Demetz, Peter. *Postwar German Literature: A Critical Introduction.* New York: Pegasus, Western Publishing Co., Inc., 1970.

Döhl, Reinhard. "Wolfgang Koeppen." In *Deutsche Literatur seit 1945 in Einzeldarstellungen.* Ed. Dietrich Weber. Stuttgart: A. Kröner, 1968, pp. 103-29.

Durzak, Manfred, ed. *Die deutsche Literatur der Gegenwart.* Stuttgart: Reclam, 1971.

—————. *Der deutsche Roman der Gegenwart.* Stuttgart: Kohlhammer, 1971.

Dvorak, Paul Francis. "Individual Failure and Desire for Change in the Works of Wolfgang Koeppen." Diss. University of Maryland, 1973.

Erlach, Dietrich. "Wolfgang Koeppen als zeitkritischer Erzähler". Diss. Uppsala University, 1973.

Greiner, Ulrich, ed. *Über Wolfgang Koeppen.* Frankfurt am Main: Suhrkamp Verlag, 1976.

Haberkamm, Klaus. "Wolfgang Koeppen: 'Bienenstock des Teufels'—Zum naturhaftmythischen Geschichts—und Gesellschaftsbild in den Nachkriegsromanen." In *Zeitkritische Romane des 20. Jahrhunderts.* Ed. Hans Wagener. Stuttgart: Philipp Reclam, 1975, pp. 241-275..

Heissenbüttel, Helmut. "Wolfgang Koeppen—Kommentar" *Merkur,* 22 (1968), pp. 244-52.

Jens, Walter. *Melancholie und Moral: Rede auf Wolfgang Koeppen.* Stuttgart: Henry Goverts Verlag, 1963.

Koch, Manfred. *Wolfgang Koeppen: Literatur zwischen Nonkonformismus und Resignation.* Stuttgart: Kohlhammer Verlag, 1973.

Koeppen, Wolfgang. *Tauben im Gras,* Das Treibhaus, Der Tod in Rom. (Einbändige Sonderausgabe der Romane.) Stuttgart: Henry Goverts Verlag, 1969.

Linder, Christian. "Schreiben als Zustand: ein Gespräch mit Wolfgang Koeppen." In *Text + Kritik.* Ed. Heinz Ludwig Arnold. Heft 34 *Wolfgang Koeppen.* München: Edition Text und Kritik, 1972, pp. 14-32.

Love, Ursula. "Wolfgang Koeppens Nachkriegstrilogie: Struktur und Erzähltechnik." Diss. Brown University, 1974.

Quack, Josef. "Die Haltung des Beobachters: Pauschale Überlegungen zu Wolfgang Koeppen." *Frankfurter Hefte,* 29. Jahrgang, Heft 11 (1974), pp. 823-34.

Rasch, Wolfdietrich. "Wolfgang Koeppen." In *Deutsche Dichter der Gegenwart.* Ed. Benno von Wiese. Berlin: Erich Schmidt Verlag, 1973, pp. 210-230.

Reich-Ranicki, Marcel. "Der Fall Wolfgang Koeppen." In *Über Wolfgang Koeppen*. Ed. Ulrich Greiner. Frankfurt am Main: Suhrkamp, 1976, pp. 101-08.

──────. "Der Zeuge Koeppen" In *Über Wolfgang Koeppen*. Ed. Ulrich Greiner. ed. Frankfurt am Main: Suhrkamp, 1976, pp. 133-50.

Vormweg, Heinrich. "Deutsche Literatur 1945-1960." In *Die Deutsche Literatur der Gegenwart*. Ed. Manfred Durzak. Stuttgart: Reclam, 1971, pp. 13-30.

Weber, Dietrich, ed. *Deutsche Literatur seit 1945 in Einzeldarstellungen*. Stuttgart: A. Kröner, 1968.

Wiese, Benno von. "Literarisches Porträt des Schriftstellers Wolfgang Koeppen." *Die Zeit*, 21.4.1967.

Index